ONE BUCKET AT A TIME

A WOMAN'S GUIDE TO CREATING WEALTH

Start Filling Your
Money Buckets!

D. Terrell

ONE
BUCKET
AT A
TIME

A WOMAN'S GUIDE TO CREATING WEALTH

TERRELL DINKINS

BOOKLOGIX®
Alpharetta, GA

Copyright © 2015 by Terrell Dinkins

All rights reserved. No part of this book may be reproduced or transmitted in any form or by any means, electronic or mechanical, including photocopying, recording, or any information storage and retrieval system, without permission in writing from the publisher. For more information, address BookLogix, c/o Permissions Department, 1264 Old Alpharetta Rd., Alpharetta, GA 30005.

ISBN: 978-1-61005-706-6
Library of Congress Control Number: 2015919219

10 9 8 7 6 5 4 3 2   0 4 0 6 1 7

Printed in the United States of America

∞This paper meets the requirements of ANSI/NISO Z39.48-1992 (Permanence of Paper)

To women who have potential for financial greatness
but fall victim to themselves and the unknowns of wealth building

Contents

Foreword   ix

Acknowledgments   xi

Introduction   Wealth Building Is a Journey   xiii

Chapter 1   Why Women?   1

Chapter 2   Facing the Woman in the Mirror   15

Chapter 3   Creating Your Spending Plan (The Budget)   31

Chapter 4   What's in Your Money Buckets?   45

Chapter 5   Protecting Your Buckets   73

Chapter 6   If Money Wasn't an Object   85

Chapter 7   Terrell's Personal Top Ten Wealth-Building Tips   89

Epilogue   Lessons for Generations   95

Appendix A   Common Monthly Expenditures & Outflows   99

Appendix B   Personal Balance Sheet   103

Appendix C   Debt Ratios   105

Bibliography   107

About the Author   109

Foreword

THE LIGHT IS DIMMING ON THE FINANCIAL FUTURE FOR WOMEN. THE majority of us aren't saving enough money to support our retirement years, and many of us will have to work past the age of seventy if we continue to save at our current dismal rate. When was the last time you sat and asked yourself this important question: "If I did nothing to change my relationship with my money, would I have enough to reach my future goals?" If your answer is "No," then you have picked up the right book. Fundamentally, we understand what wealth is, but how to get there has been somewhat of a mystery—until now.

In *One Bucket at a Time: A Woman's Guide to Creating Wealth*, Terrell shows us how to get what she refers to as "calm wealth" that can't be quantified with a dollar amount. How refreshing is it to know that wealth has less to do with the amount of money you have but everything to do with the type of lifestyle that you want to live today and in the future? Terrell delivers a practical approach to building wealth using her "bucket system."

I'll never forget our first meeting, as we sat in the conference room of her office, and she began drawing buckets on an electronic board. Each bucket represented how we should think about our money. By the time she got to the third bucket, I said, "That's it. You have to write a book!" Thank you, Terrell, for acting on my advice. This life-changing book will get so many women on the right path to creating sustainable wealth.

For many years, I've built my wealth through building businesses and investing in real estate, yet I've always understood the importance of having a qualified financial advisor, a person to help me diversify my portfolio of assets and look for ways to grow my money. I've always been intrigued with wealth building and loved the concept of the Rule of 72, which shows how long it would take to double your money at a given interest rate. I refer to compound interest as the eighth wonder of the world. As I think about the things that I have done to build wealth, I realize that the number one way I reached my financial goals was through my mindset. Knowing what you want and keeping your mind focused on your goals is 90 percent of the battle. Wealth building comes down to making what seems to be a present sacrifice for a future gain. And over time, you will strengthen your wealth-building muscle and see your money buckets begin to grow.

As your vision for your life, your children, your future, and your choices becomes clearer, the process of filling your money buckets will become easier and eventually overflow. Not only will you have enough for your lifetime, but for your generation and future generations to come. The impact of the sacrifices you make during your lifetime will resonate loud and clear in your legacy.

Happy wealth building,
Sonia Booker, "The Wealthbuilder"
Entrepreneur, Author, Speaker

Acknowledgments

I WOULD LIKE TO THANK GOD FOR ALLOWING ME TO WALK IN MY purpose and find my voice. Not many people can say they know why they were placed on this earth, but I can. The saying, "Find out what you are willing and love to do for free and pursue that for a life full of peace and happiness," could not be truer in my case. When you tap into this space, you have found your purpose. Helping others reach their "Aha!" moment with their finances brings me so much joy. All of my life, I knew I was meant to help others with their money. I personally never felt comfortable when I wasn't on top of my own finances. When my financial house is in order, I am at peace. I want others to feel this way about their money and finances.

Sonia Booker, thank you so much for saying, "You have a book in you and people need to hear your message." Boy, were those words flattering. Talk about one woman empowering another! The nudge you gave me catapulted my thinking to the next level. Words cannot express my gratitude for your unselfish support and belief in my abilities to help others with my money buckets message.

Sharon Frame, I appreciate your guidance and words of encouragement. You put an inspirational fire under me and helped me push through the initial hurdle of getting started on my manuscript.

Candice Bovian, thanks for keeping me accountable to deadlines. The weekly phone calls and reports of my progress truly helped me push through moments when I didn't feel like writing.

Jeff, my beloved husband, thank you for always supporting me. You have never complained about my many entrepreneurial ventures. Having you has made being a mother, wife, and entrepreneur easy.

Listening to you has allowed me to see other people's circumstances in a different perspective. I truly appreciate your insight.

Jeffrey and Jordan, I didn't forget about you two. I find it humbling that you have seen the success of my dreams in your dreams. You have continuously encouraged me to dream big. Such wise thoughts for young minds. Saying that you admire me only makes me want to do bigger and better things in life. The sky is the limit for all of us.

I'd also like to thank the women who have shared their stories and allowed me to see parts of their lives that continue to be a financial struggle. Some were never taught how to create wealth or never had role models that were examples of wealth builders. Nonetheless, I am inspired by the professional women that I encounter daily who want to see a more comfortable and secure future. You provide fuel to my purpose.

Introduction
Wealth Building Is a Journey

I WAS NOT BORN INTO MONEY, NOR HAVE I EVER INHERITED A DIME. I used to be intrigued by the behavior of those with money and those I *thought* had money. As a young child, I was no different than most people. I dreamed about what it would feel like to live in a mansion or drive a two-seater red sports car. A world with no financial limits often ran across my youthful mind. Now that I am older and much wiser, the only thing that runs across my mind in reference to a big mansion is how long it would take to clean it and the cost to upkeep such an elaborate lifestyle.

When you think about the levels of wealth displayed in our society, you have those who are quite pretentious, making sure the world sees their wealth. They drive the fancy cars I dreamed about as a child, wear the finest tailored clothing, and carry the latest in designer handbags. As you become more aware, you quickly learn that many of those very individuals are barely getting by financially. They are in deep debt and struggling to stay afloat.

Then you have those who never appear wealthy but always manage to come up with money when it is needed most. These people keep you guessing about how much money they actually have. They appear to be calm when handling their wealth. One of their cars of choice is usually a modestly priced American-made sedan. Their appearance fits the characteristics described in Thomas Stanley's *The Millionaire Next Door*, which describes how most common millionaires live simple lives and do not show off their wealth.[1]

---

[1] Thomas J. Stanley, *The Millionaire Next Door*. (Lanham, MD: Taylor Trade Publishing, 2010).

My first job out of college was as a Branch Operations Manager/ Personal Banker for First Atlanta Bank, which is now Wells Fargo. Sitting in my office during slow business hours at the bank, I would play the guessing game with those who walked in the branch. Yes, I was judging the book by its cover, trying to predict a person's financial status. I had an office with a window, which allowed me to see the cars that came in and out of the bank's parking lot. I got pretty good at the guessing game and quickly learned some of the stories of how people came into their wealth, especially those who were referred to me by the bank tellers.

For those who were really wealthy, I learned that it took years of saving and watching their spending habits closely, even down to the last penny. Many of the older wealthy women who didn't like the stock market placed their money in certificates of deposit (back in the early nineties, rates were over 5½ percent). CDs and savings bonds were very safe places to keep your money. Bank clients would live off of the interest on the CDs (unfortunately, I don't think we will see those days again for a very long time).

From my short time at one particular branch, one story stays with me even today. One of the women who frequented the branch came to me one day and asked if I could help her balance her checkbook. I found her request odd. I always saw her coming in with her two small children, making deposits or cashing checks. We always exchanged pleasantries, and I knew she was married to a Delta pilot. I discovered that her life was about to change. Her husband had asked her for a divorce and she was suddenly going to be thrust into unfamiliar territory—money management. During her entire marriage, her husband handled all of the household finances. She was going to be on her own financially and raising two children nearly on her own. I felt really sad for this woman. I vowed never to find myself under these circumstances and to do what I could to help those in similar situations.

The stories of so many people I encountered in my banking years brought me to realize that building wealth was going to be a journey for me. I never thought I would be a wealthy person who lived in a mansion. Nope, that was never my dream. I knew I wanted to live a very comfortable life, and I didn't want to worry about money. I liked how calm those who had accumulated wealth appeared. I wanted what they had, a calm wealth that couldn't be quantified with a particular dollar amount. For me, calm wealth looked like a house on a hill, two children, a husband, family vacations, travel, and relaxation during my retirement years. Family vacations were a must because I never had them growing up as a child. I remember hearing my dad discussing with my mother how he wanted to buy a van and take us to Disney World, but that trip never happened. My dad died at the age of thirty-six from a heart attack. My first trip to Disney World was thirty years later when I was a mother to my two children.

I have never prayed for a particular sum of money. To be honest, as far as I can remember, I've felt that praying for a particular sum of money sets limits on God's infinite possibilities. What I did do was dream and imagine what my life would be like in various situations. I've always had a vision of myself in a blue suit, a baby on one hip, and a briefcase in my other hand. This has been my reality on so many occasions. I never wanted to be a stay-at-home mom. I wanted to be a mom who went after her dream of becoming a business woman. This is my reality now.

Our visions can become our reality and one of the first steps to achieving your financial goals begins with building wealth in smart and responsible ways.

Humans are visual creatures. You can tell people how to do something, and they just might be a bit confused, but once you *show* them, the message resonates in their minds and they remember what you've taught them. So I'm going to show you an image to focus on and learn from. I'm sure you've heard the saying, "A drop in the bucket," which means a small amount compared to what is necessary. I want my readers to visualize their finances categorized in money buckets. I don't want you to end up with only a drop in your buckets when expenses are due, or you are retiring, or when you have children. The goal is to fill as many of the four money buckets as early in life as possible. Time is truly a friend when you are building wealth. Each of the four buckets has a purpose and will be utilized throughout different stages of your life.

As an advisor, I have found that when people operate out of one pile of money (a single bucket) they never reach their goals. Murphy's Law—anything that can go wrong, will go wrong—always seems to kick in and deplete their pile of cash. The simple movement of your money in and out of one account can't get you where you want to go.

Because of inflation and time, the buckets cannot look the same and must serve different purposes (I will delve into the options you have for each bucket under the chapter "What's in Your Money Buckets?"). For the purposes of this book, I will concentrate on the four main money buckets every person should try to generate in their lifetime: Short-Term, Midterm, Long-Term, and Guaranteed.

Before we fill our money buckets in the final chapters of the book, I think it is important that we look at the habits that prevent us from building wealth, despite the fact that we live in a world of milk and honey. Women have a huge opportunity to close the money gaps we see between men and women. More women have entered the workforce, and there is a campaign in America to close the disparity in pay between men and women. I have hope that change is coming if we make noise and let our voices be heard. For this reason—and the fact that most of my clients are professional women—I have firsthand knowledge of the opportunities in this group.

Women are making strides in the workforce. They are making money, despite the heavily-debated pay gap between men and women in our country. Not everyone will create a million-dollar net worth (assets minus liabilities equals net worth), but they can build wealth. I am convinced that we can have more millionaires in our country, especially among the professional women that I see in my practice. Those who have good incomes truly have a shot at achieving millionaire status without winning the lottery or inventing the next big product. We can and should see more families and individuals with a positive net worth. Many people—with time on their side and behavioral changes—can reach this dream and live a comfortable life in retirement, without making huge sacrifices before they get there.

The first chapter of this book will take a closer look at the opportunities women have to build wealth and why they should start now and not later because of the specific disadvantages many of them will face in their lifetimes.

I am sure many women are asking themselves, "Can I really accumulate a million dollars or a net worth of a million dollars?" The answer is "Yes!" Some will have an easier time than others, but absolutely. Wealth building is about time and behavior. You need both to be a successful wealth builder. The earlier you start, the greater your chances. Because of this fact, I hope I will encourage young professionals who enter the workforce and land good salaries to create healthy money habits before they go on big spending sprees. If you are not a do-it-yourself type when it comes to finances, seek professional help as soon as possible so that a spending plan is put in place.

Let's look at the plain simple math of one million dollars. Fifty-thousand dollars saved per year over twenty years is $1 million. We are not talking interest, returns, income, or anything like this. This is simple multiplication: $50,000 x 20 years = $1,000,000. What about $33,333 saved per year over a thirty-year period? This also gets you to one million dollars.

Now, let's add a few returns to make this goal even more simplified. If you begin with $10,000 at the very young age of twenty-five and save $453.33 per month—the annual maximum contribution for a Roth or Traditional IRA is $5,500 per year—and it grows 6 percent a year, by the time you reach sixty-five years old, you will have $1 million. As a matter of fact, because of compounding interest, making the contribution monthly instead of annually, the total amount will be slightly more than $1 million. If you take this same amount ($453.33 per month) and contribute to your company 401(k) plan and the employer makes a fifty percent match to your contribution, with the same rate of return of 6 percent, you will amass nearly $1.5 million by the time you reach sixty-five. You don't have to make a million dollars to create a million dollars. You only have to stay the course and remain focused on your plan.

I once had an individual share that she made a combined $250,000 a year. This included salary and bonus. She explained that she lived off half of her income and had been at this level of income for several years, yet she had only saved $24,000 in a savings account earning less than 1 percent interest. Mind you, this person had opportunities to invest in her company retirement account, but she hadn't done so in the six years she had been employed there. Even with taxes taken out at the highest tax bracket for this level of income (33 percent), this individual should have had way more than $24,000 in a savings account. My heart sank when I heard what this person had saved. I was screaming on the inside and asking, "What are you doing with your money if you only live off half of what you make?"

After listening further to the story, I knew her behavioral issues would continue to prevent her from building wealth and achieving millionaire status. Making $250,000 a year in income, living in a city like Atlanta, and being young, one should clearly become a millionaire! But this behavior is not unusual, even if it's an extraordinary case of lost opportunities for wealth building. Your income doesn't have to be as high as $250,000 to become a millionaire or even to build a positive net worth.

Here's my frustration and the reason why I decided to write this book. I live in a city booming with successful young female profession-als who make six-figure incomes yet have few funds to show for their hard work. They are the ones who could reach millionaire status. How can they do it? I will say over and over again that the key to wealth building is behavior and time (mainly behavior).

I am not trying to create ultra-rich individuals. As a matter of fact, the ultra-rich (the top 0.01 percent) would hardly flinch at reaching millionaire status. I just want to see more people build a positive net worth. I want those who have the means to do so to become millionaires because this kind of wealth opens a world of opportunities to their children and them. They have the opportunity to create generational wealth!

On March 26, 2015, I attended an event hosted by an organization called the National Sales Network, and the guest speaker was Dr. Dennis Kimbro. He was a phenomenal speaker and I was quite positively moved by his presentation. According to his research spanning from 2006-2013, which is presented in his book, *The Wealth Choice: Success Secrets of Black Millionaires,* there were only 35,000 individual African Americans (roughly .01 percent of the U.S. population) "who possess a net worth of $1 million or more."[2] Two years after his book had been published, the numbers had not changed. I have yet to find any data to dispute his findings. I was very disappointed to learn these statistics.

Even if these numbers are not exactly correct—I doubt any institution is able to capture all of the financial facts from every household in the United States—there is still cause to be concerned that too few of us are reaching millionaire status. Our future of wealth building seems bleak, but there is still hope for those who want help.

As an African-American woman, I think we can exceed the 35,000 individuals Dr. Kimbro found in his research, and I think we must start with women because they are changing the face of the workplace and the family dynamics. More than ever, women in this country are the "bread winners" in their households. They are landing powerful jobs

---

[2] Dennis P. Kimbro, *The Wealth Choice: Success Secrets of Black Millionaires,* (New York, NY: Palgrave Macmillan, 2013).

and starting to find their places in the boardrooms. Their journeys to wealth will be long ones, though still obtainable if they begin before they start families, before they spend all of their money shopping for material possessions that lose value, before they become caregivers, or before they become wives. I want to show women how to get there, starting now, **one bucket at a time**.

NOTES

Chapter 1
Why Women?

Longevity

WOMEN ARE BORN WITH A BLESSING AND A CURSE. ON AVERAGE, WE outlive our male counterparts by almost five years. As a matter of fact, some of us will live long past the ripe old age of one hundred and be placed in the category of a centenarian (a person who lives to or beyond one hundred). Just imagine living long enough to see generations of family members prosper and grow. I personally hope I inherit the longevity gene that's in my family (my maternal grandmother turned ninety-five years old the summer of 2015, and our family celebrated this wondrous occasion).

According to reporting done by *USA Today*, "Life expectancy in the USA rose in 2012 to 78.8 years . . . according to a new report on mortality in the USA from the Centers for Disease Control and Prevention's National Center for Health Statistics," and "the average life expectancy for a person who was 65 years old in 2012 is 19.3 years—20.5 years for women and 17.9 years for men."[3] If you poll all of your friends, I am sure they can identify a family member or someone they know who has lived to reach one hundred. For this reason, I think it is wise that all retirement planning should span at least thirty years if you decide to retire at sixty-five.

Longevity can be a beautiful thing if you have a sound mind and have prepared financially for the journey. Imagine still traveling and seeing the world well into your seventies and eighties. With the advancement in

---

[3] Larry Copeland, "Life Expectancy in the USA Hits a Record High," *USA Today*, Oct. 9, 2014, http://www.usatoday.com/story/new/nation/2014/10/08/us-life-expectancy-hits-recor-high/16874039.

medicine and technology, this is still quite possible. It's not unreasonable to consider sixty-five "mid-life," especially if you still have thirty years ahead of you.

So is it fair to use the word curse to describe longevity? One of the biggest fears of the elderly is outliving their money and having to rely on others for financial support. Add to that the stress of loneliness often associated with being a widow, and you might consider longevity a curse. Who ends up being old, lonely, and broke? More often than not it's us, women.[4] Gender inequality doesn't end with our paychecks. For many women, the gender gap haunts them into their retirement years when they live alone.

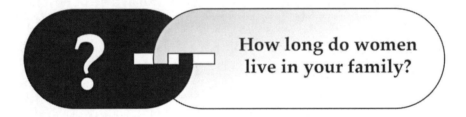

How long do women live in your family?

Widowhood

Becoming a widow is one of life's tragedies that so many women will, unfortunately, face in their lifetimes. Many people intuitively think this is something that happens after a long life together with a spouse, but this isn't always so. Statistics show that a third of people who become widows are younger than the age of sixty. According to the US Census, variation rates of widowhood between men and women can be attributed to gender differences in marriage.[5] Women live longer than men and tend to marry older men, which consequently results in widowhood. The

---

[4] Melanie Hicken, "Why Many Retired Women Live in Poverty," *CNN Money*, May 13, 2014, http://money.cnn.com/2014/05/13/retirement/retirement-women/.
[5] Diana B. Elliott and Tavia Simmons, "Marital Events of Americans: 2009," *United States Census Bureau*, Aug. 2011, https://www.census.gov/prod/2011pubs/acs-13.pdf.

woman is more likely to live alone after the death of a spouse and subsequently have higher per capita household expenses. Men, on the other hand, are statistically more likely to remarry after the loss of a spouse through divorce or death.

My own mother became a widow at the young age of thirty-four. She had three children to raise alone. I was ten when my father passed away, and my mother did not remarry until I turned twenty-six. As a child, I could not imagine anyone taking my father's place, despite the fact that my mother had a very difficult time managing the load of motherhood and widowhood. She made the choice to not get married again until her children were adults. This decision to raise a family alone takes a huge financial toll on a person's ability to save money unless there are financial plans in place, such as large sums of life insurance or other financial assets that will make the family financially sound after the death of a spouse. This wasn't the case for my family. Because my mother was a young widow with three children under the age of eighteen, the Social Security system extended a safety net to cover my family until my youngest sister graduated from high school. This safety net allowed my mother time to grieve, which I believe lasted for many years, judging by the number of nights I heard her crying.

For many women, the road to poverty begins after the death of their husbands. The loss of income in the household only gets worse. Those who haven't prepared for the worst but have accumulated savings often find their savings wiped out, trying to cover living expenses on a single income instead of two. I tell my clients all the time, "Tragedy never makes an appointment with you. Tragedy comes knocking when you least expect it. Be prepared when it does."

A Man Is Not a Plan

Many women during the mid-twentieth century were taught that when they left college, in addition to earning a regular degree, they needed to also return home with an MRS (Mrs.) degree. As antiquated as this may sound today, many women still wish for this. Many still want their knight in shining armor to come along and sweep them away. Many women hate to admit it, but they want protection and someone to take care of them.

Today, I know women who have earned degrees and made the decision to put their careers on hold to take on the extremely difficult role of the stay-at-home mother. I am saddened, however, when I hear some of them say, "I have no idea what my husband has put in place financially for the family. He takes care of the finances and pays all of the bills." The household roles are great if they have been agreed upon collectively, but disturbing if she doesn't know what is going on with the household finances. A blank stare should not be the response when you ask about a spousal IRA or if the husband has life insurance in the event of his untimely death. If you have decided to take on the role of a homemaker, make sure you are knowledgeable about the finances of your home. You do not have to be an expert. There are people who can help you with that part. Just know what you have in place and how to get your hands on it in the event you are suddenly faced with running your household alone.

Even in the role of the stay-at-home mom, your man should not be your final plan. Here's why! Many couples end up in divorce court, and much is lost during divorce. Starting over is not easy. The degree you earned many moons ago has most likely become outdated. While you were at home taking care of your children, you failed to take care of your technical skills. Please do not misconstrue what I am saying. I am not dooming your marriage. I do believe in happily-ever-after. Women just need to be smart and keep their eyes wide open about their circumstances.

Use some of your downtime while you are home to think about what you love to do. I am sure many of you said, "What down time?" after reading that sentence. I firmly believe that we make time for what we want. So again, create some downtime in your schedule and really focus on your strengths. Think about those gifts that come naturally and effortlessly. Things you would do for free if money wasn't an issue. Trust me, this will come in handy one day.

As far as those women who never earned their so called "MRS" Degree during their college years, make sure you think long-term and don't live your life constantly thinking about the immediate ifs: "If I buy myself a house, I might scare off a guy," or "If I save too much money, he might feel intimidated about how much I have in the bank." Live your life with joy and keep in the back of your mind that it might only be you flying solo. You may have to be the one taking care of yourself for the rest of your life. If that is the case, don't blow all of your money on possessions. Have fun, but be smart. If and when he comes along, he will appreciate you for you and all you have accomplished. He won't be the solution to your plan, but he will be a part of the plan.

Our Seat at the Table

Just like women want men to be a part of their plan, we are living in an age where men want an equal partner in a relationship. Are you in a position to be an equal partner? Have you gotten your house in order so that you are not going into a relationship with financial baggage? What are you bringing to the table? I am sure men would feel this is a fair question. So many men are fed up with women who are looking for a knight in shining armor. Women may want to be rescued, but men don't always want to rescue them.

Let me clarify by saying that when I write "equal partner," I mean in financial knowledge and participation. You do not need to make a six-figure income if he also makes a good salary. That would be great for the household financially, but that is not what I mean by equal partnership. I am referring to both people in the marriage taking an equal stake in the financial affairs, literally and mentally.

Entering into a relationship with something to offer is important. You may not make a great deal of money, but you can bring value when it comes to handling money. I know a couple who has been married for over twenty-five years, and the husband confessed to me that he and his wife have a great business partnership. I didn't know how to take his confession because he sounded like he wanted to say, "It was cheaper to keep her." But I listened anyway. He said he would never leave his wife because he trusted her with his money, and he knew that his bills would be paid on time. They both worked outside of the home, and their paychecks weren't equal, but they both had something to bring to the table. In her situation, it was her ability to handle their finances.

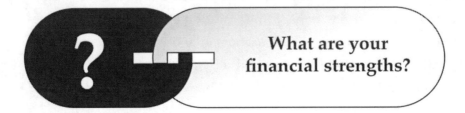

? What are your financial strengths?

Men who know they have something to offer watch women's every move. They observe how we handle money. The smart ones think deeper than simply obtaining a trophy for their arms. If he is going places, he wants a good woman who can help him get there. He wants someone who can elevate him and take him to the next level. They think about the future just like we do.

If you are dealing with shopping demons, get rid of them. If you have purchased a designer handbag or a pair of shoes that cost more than what is sitting in your savings account, you may be dealing with a shopping demon, especially if spending like that is a habit. I have heard far too many times a woman justifying the expensive purchase because she thinks she deserves it because she works hard. Well, you deserve a better future for yourself, and you could possibly be running off a potential mate because you have an issue with spending. Rid yourself of the thirst for material possessions. It might be stopping you from having an equal voice, an equal space, and a seat next to your mate.

Sandwich Generation

Let me describe a scenario for you. You get up before sunrise to make your children breakfast and get them dressed and off to the bus stop. Then you head to the office. You work all day, head home, and then find yourself stuck in traffic, hoping you will make it in time to pick up your children from their after-school program before you are fined again. You get the children home, fed, and bathed. Their homework is completed. But your day does not end here. You call your sitter to come over while you leave to relieve the nurse who has been hired to watch your mother during the day. When you arrive to your mother's home, the nurse reminds you that she has not been paid.

This is a dilemma that I've heard over and over from many clients who are caring for a parent with their siblings. They often miss major aspects of their family's activities because it is their turn to stay the weekend with their parent who can't afford full-time in-home nursing care. The cost of part-time care for their parent is split among the siblings, but this additional expense still creates an added financial burden on their households.

Does this story sound familiar? Many adults, especially women, are caught in a quandary, raising their own children and becoming a caregiver to their aging parents. They are called the "Sandwich Generation" because they are sandwiched into caring for the generations before and after their own.[6] These burdens often still fall on the shoulders of the women in families. They are drained of their time, money, energy, and job opportunities. Caregiving seems to be a black mark on their job resumes. When women leave the workforce prematurely for childcare and eldercare, they leave money on the table. This money includes future raises and reduced Social Security benefits, which is often the only pension they will ever receive. The days of staying at a company

---

[6] Kim Parker and Eileen Patten, "The Sandwich Generation: Rising Financial Burdens for Middle-Aged Americans," *Pew Research Center*, Jan. 30, 2013, http://www.pewsocialtrends.org/2013/01/30/the-sandwich-generation/.

until you retire and receiving full pension benefits are long gone. I suspect the word "pension" will soon become obsolete, just like a cassette tape. I am sure someone reading this book is asking, "What's a cassette tape?" Exactly.

Who's caring for the caregiver? Often these groups of individuals neglect themselves. Being a healthy and well-rested caregiver is a gift and blessing to those you love. Many books are written specifically to provide recommendations aimed at taking care of the caregiver.[7] Here's a summary of tips by Dr. Ruth Tarantine to help those who are stuck in difficult caregiving situations (consult other resources for more in-depth guidance): 1) Be kind to yourself and accept help when it is offered. 2) Take breaks when you can. 3) Keep a bag of essentials—books, lotion, your favorite music—on hand at all times. 4) Live a healthy lifestyle by eating well and avoiding alcohol and caffeine. 5) Try to find counseling help or join a support group. 6) Find the joy in life when you can. Laughter will lift the soul.[8]

Closing the Pay Gap

Pay gaps between men's and women's salaries have been an issue since women entered the workforce. Even if we don't close this gap, women can better prepare themselves in how they build wealth for retirement and a long life.

According to *Forbes*, "Women make up nearly half the U.S. workforce, receive more college degrees than men, and are the sole breadwinners in four of ten American households. Yet, they earn less than men at virtually every job—a persistent problem known as the gender pay gap. And

---

[7] Ruth A. Tarantine, *Against All Odds: How to Move from Provider-Centered Care to Patient-Centered Care*, (Pittsburgh, PA: inCredible Messages Press, 2014).
[8] Ruth Tarantine, "The Sandwich Generation: Who Is Caring for You?" *The Huffington Post*, Sept. 7, 2014, http://www.huffingtonpost.com/ruth-tarantine-dnp-rn/baby-boomers-caregivers_b_5733782.html.

that gap can mean a more challenging retirement for women."[9] These numbers are more astounding among women in the African-American community. And according to *Retirement and Good Living*, "Women enter retirement with less saved due to a lifetime of lower earnings. The average pay for a woman is just seventy-seven cents for every dollar earned by a man, and even less for black and Hispanic women. The Center for American Progress estimates that over the average working woman's forty-year career, this difference may add up to $431,000."[10]

While the pay gap remains a huge debate, especially in how to close it, women have been consistently accruing a larger and larger share of the pie. According to reporting done by WealthManagement.com taken from a TD Ameritrade Institutional study, "Women currently control $8 trillion in assets in the US, a figure that is expected to jump to $22 trillion by 2020. [Fidelity reports in its] most recent Millionaire Outlook, roughly 40 percent of women out-earn their spouses."[11] If I took a survey of most of the women I know, this percentage would probably hold true, especially for those who work in corporate America.

Well, if we don't close the money gap, what can we do to improve our financial situation now and in retirement? The answer is to take a new and different approach to retirement planning. Here are some suggestions on how to get creative and find solutions for wealth building.

---

[9] Divya Raghavan, "How the Gender Pay Gap Harms Women's Retirement," *Forbes*, Nov. 12, 2014, http://www.forbes.com/sites/nextavenue/2014/11/12/how-the-gender-pay-gap-harms-women.

[10] Donna M. Phelan, "Women's New Retirement Conversation," *Retirement and Good Living*, Feb. 17, 2015, http://retirementandgoodliving.com/womens-news-retirement-conversation/.

[11] Cindy Scott, "Meeting the Financial Planning Needs of Women Clients," WealthManagement.com, Jan. 23, 2014, http://wealthmanagement.com/viewpoints/meeting-financial-planning-needs-women-clients.

1. **Create multiple streams of income and stack your cash in your money buckets that I will cover later in the book.** One way to increase your cash flow is to get a part-time job. Before I got married and had children, I didn't know what it was like to only work one job. I always had a side gig going. Turn one of your hobbies into a home-based business by using your God-given skills, tools, and talents.

2. **Relocate to a state with a lower cost of living.** Let's face it, you can live a more affordable lifestyle in Atlanta than you can in Manhattan. Every time I visit New York, I get excited about the fast pace, hustle and bustle, the make-it-happen-now mentality, until I step inside an apartment that costs more to rent than my mortgage.

3. **Stack more money in your retirement accounts, especially if you are not meeting your company match!** If you qualify for a Roth account, add to that in addition to your company match, provided you are not saving too much for later and struggling to meet current living expenses.

4. **Get a roommate!** During the housing bubble, many people purchased "McMansions" and are still paying the price for their dream homes. If you live alone, rent out one of your rooms to a friend. I met one woman who finished her basement and converted it into a very nice apartment. Consider non-traditional residence sharing as a great way to build your nest egg.

5. **I've been telling my girlfriend for years that she should delay retirement and work longer.** Even if she takes on a part-time job, the delay will give her more time to build her nest egg. If you continue to stay busy, it keeps your

mind active. Because we are living longer, our retirement nest eggs will need to be larger than we think.

6. **Make your money work for you.** Instead of reinvesting capital gains and dividends from stocks and mutual funds, have the money come to you. There is no rule that says you should always reinvest your capital gains. The gains made can assist with your cash flow and will likely cost you less if you are in a lower income tax bracket during retirement.

7. **Start filling your guarantee bucket, which I will cover in more detail later, by creating income for life.** Some annuities may provide income that is guaranteed by the insurance company to be deposited in your bank account for the rest of your life. This income could be used for travel, leisure, or even assisting a grandchild with tuition, if that is your pleasure. When my IRA reached a certain level, I transferred some of the money into an annuity. I like the thought of guarantees.

The time to act on building wealth is now. Be creative and seek help if you don't know how to get started.

Women Are Intuitive

Let's face it. Women know when something is not right, especially when it comes to their finances. Just doing my own mental survey of the husband and wife clients in my practice, I have found that it is often the wife who makes the first move to seek out financial help through an advisor. In many cases, several discussions are had at home before she lands in my office. She makes the phone call and the first visit before dragging her spouse to the office. This was even the case in my own personal situation when my husband and I were in the process of getting our wills and power of attorney completed. We went back and forth on guardianship—which was the holdup—and I finally made the move to see an attorney. Not having a will in place and having minor children ate at my gut for years. I vowed that before I gave any advice to clients, I would make sure my house was in order. I hate to see people saying, "Do as I say and not as I do." That was not going to be me.

When it comes to money and households, most women will consider themselves the decision makers. This could be because they pay the bills and run the household finances. Again, according to reporting done by WealthManagement.com, "A 2011 study from Prudential, 'Financial Experience and Behaviors among Women,' revealed that some 95 percent of women are directly involved in their households' financial decisions and 25 percent stated that they were the primary decision-maker."[12] This seems contradictory, but it isn't. We recognize that we need help, especially with more complicated financial issues like retirement planning, but we don't know where or how to start. Most of my female clients who are interested in planning know how to save money the old fashion way but are hesitant in taking on risk that will build wealth beyond inflationary rates. This hesitation could stem from the fact that we make less than our male counterparts and don't want to take on as much risk.

I have found that barriers to risk dissipate if there is a respect in how facts are communicated. Women communicate differently than men, and we want to feel secure. Security has to co-exist in our financial decision-making process. Women want to learn in a welcoming environment broken down in plain English. We need the picture painted.

---

[12] Cindy Scott, "Meeting the Financial Planning Needs of Women Clients."

NOTES

Chapter 2

Facing the Woman in the Mirror

A Borrower Is a Slave to Her Lender

WHO DO YOU OWE? WHO HAS BONDAGE OVER YOU? WHAT KEEPS YOU up at night: MasterCard, Visa, or American Express? Before wealth building begins, you need to write a list of who you are indebted to. This step is the most difficult but the most important part of building a financial plan. It takes courage. You will discover so much about your spending habits. It might be quite an eye-opening experience for you.

I met a woman who shared with me that she did not have any credit card debt. She paid her credit cards off when they came in. On the surface, this looked great, but here's what she discovered. When conducting the exercise of writing out a budget and listing all credit card debt and monthly expenditures, even though she paid the cards off in full every month, her spending was out of control, to the tune of well over $150,000 per year. This woman earned more than $300,000 per year, yet she had saved less than $50,000. She was enslaved to the "Swipe." She swiped her charge card every time she thought she was getting a good deal. She felt even better about herself when she paid off the bill. But guess how disappointed she was when she found out she had not accumulated more wealth. It's important to ask: Is this you?

Here's what I want you to do this month. If you picked up this book, you have shown some interest in changing your financial future and building wealth, right? We are going to make this process as simple as possible. If you are a technology buff, you can use the notes app on your phone. You can decide on the method. What's important is you face your reality. For every credit card statement and loan that comes through your mailbox this month write out/type out 1) what you owe (the balance), 2) your monthly payments, 3) the interest rate, and 4) how long it will take you to pay off the credit card if you make the payment suggestion shown on the statement. Once you are done, you should have four columns on your paper or computer.

What You Owe	The Intrest Rate	Your Monthly	Pay Off
The Balance		Payments	If Payments are Made as Suggested

The problem with most people is they do not pay attention to the details shown on their credit card statement. They make the minimum payment and neglect the rest of the balance. Once you've filled out the four columns for credit card debt, and you find that it will take you until you reach retirement to pay off a small credit card bill, you will probably think twice about the amount you are paying (and maybe how much you are spending). As long as you are a borrower, someone else will hold you captive financially and mentally. How does that make you feel? We should position ourselves to be in a position of strength. Become a lender and not a borrower.

And don't fool yourself if you are paying the card off each month. This is better than making the minimum payments but not at the expense of building wealth. You will never be able to pay yourself first if you must constantly pay the credit card companies each time you get your paycheck.

Wealth Is a Behavior

All of my life, my mother has told me, "It's not how much you make, but what you do with what you make that separates 'the haves' from the 'have nots.'" I have encountered many individuals who seem to have it all, materially, until you pull back the curtain to discover that they really are "have nots" on paper. Most of their possessions are depreciable things with little to show in appreciable assets.

Before we can begin the process of wealth building, we must first examine and face our own spending habits. What is driving your continued lack of prosperity? Is it a mindset? Do you say to yourself, "I work hard so I deserve to buy whatever I want, when I choose?" Could it be that you grew up in a household and learned unhealthy spending habits? Are you influenced by your social circles or the media? Do you spend to feel relevant in today's culture? Whatever the case may be, you will never build wealth if you are not disciplined to do so. It takes a different mindset to build wealth. You must want it and be willing to make a few sacrifices to get it.

We are now living in an age where glamour is forced upon us by the media. Everyone looks fabulous, and we want to look like the characters we see on our favorite television shows. We want to look like we live in a world filled with fantasy. The designer handbags and shoes we see worn by these characters cost a pretty penny and many of us will not stop until we can replicate the look.

Take the character Olivia Pope from the hit television show *Scandal*. Olivia dresses to perfection and never misses a fashion beat with the latest designer handbags and attire. I have often wondered, after watching the show, how is she going to take care of herself when she is older? She's a beautiful, successful, African-American woman who has reached her mid-thirties but has yet to find her "Mr. Right." Is she financially prepared for the future, perhaps a future that does not include a family or the house in Vermont which her character so desperately yearns for? Many professional women I know could probably identify with her (minus all of the scandal surrounding her life, including her affair with the US president).

The first thing you must throw out of the window is the instant gratification mindset. I am here to tell you that the average person will not become wealthy overnight unless they hit the lottery. Even in the case of lottery winners, many of them lose their riches when they are not in the right financial mindset. I am sure you have seen the television shows that examine how lottery winners have all lost their millions in a short period of time. We even see this with athletes and entertainers who seem to have it all at the height of their careers only to lose it all because of reckless spending habits and poor money management.

Wealth building for the average worker is a slow, steady, and methodical process. You must have a plan in place. Those who become wealthy all stick to their plan. They create healthy spending habits.

Let's examine your spending habits and face them head-on. Here are a few questions you should ask yourself to fully understand the reasons behind your spending patterns. There are several books that delve into this subject much more deeply than we are going to go in this section, but I want you to ask yourself these questions to get a clearer understanding of your spending habits.

1. *Who Do You Spend Your Money On?*
   Is it all about you and what you deserve every time you walk into a department store? Or are you the guilty mom or aunt who feels so very fortunate because you have landed a great job and feel it is only right that you share

your fortunes with others? I have a single client who loves splurging on her nieces and nephews, especially when there is a great sale going on at her favorite department store. She treats herself but gets so much more pleasure out of treating her family. She loves buying cute outfits for the children and spending a few days a week at upscale restaurants, treating the children to high-end dining. This behavior is fine if it is occasional because we should be cheerful givers but not to the detriment of taking care of our own personal finances first. When she finally calculated how much she was spending by being a cheerful giver, she was quite shocked, especially because she discovered her wealth in financial assets was so little.

_____

_____

_____

2. *What Do You Spend Money On?*
    We all have our spending vices. Some things have an invisible price tag because no matter what the cost, we will buy. I have seen a woman drop an entire paycheck on a handbag. This is a woman who has chosen fashion over financial freedom. I am certainly not judging her, but I do have a problem when the handbag costs more than what is in her savings account!

_____

_____

_____

I will admit that at some point, I spent too many days going through the drive-through, purchasing my tall, extra-hot, nonfat green tea lattes. When I calculated that having my favorite drink five times a week cost me $904.80 per year, I abruptly put the brakes on my lattes. I cut down on the number I have per week. I was oblivious to the amount I was spending until I saw the number of times Starbucks was showing up on my credit card statement (which, by the way, I pay off in full every month). This is what we all should do. Take a look at our credit cards and debit card statements and see what you are spending your money on monthly. I took the liberty of seeing how much I could accumulate if I took my $904.80 and placed it in an account with a modest 6 percent rate of return. At the beginning of thirty years, I would have a nice nest egg of $81,568.36! Not bad for a green tea latte.

Some of us are slaves to fashion, cosmetics, dining out, entertainment, and, in my case, green tea lattes. Ask yourself this question: Is this amount of spending on my favorite thing necessary? Do I really need another handbag or a pair of shoes? Can I hold off on purchasing the latest shade of pink lipstick from the makeup counter at my favorite department store and see if I can find a similar shade at the drugstore? The cosmetics industry is huge business, and we are spending billions of dollars trying to look pretty.

3. *Where Do You Spend Money?*

Because I must try on everything I purchase, I cannot buy fashion over the internet, but many of us are quite the experts. E-commerce, which turned twenty years old in 2014, has captured a sizable amount of retail market share. Many professional women are too busy to go shopping so when they do have downtime, they turn to their mobile devices and catch the daily deals, which seem to be available on all retail sites. The convenience of the internet has widened the sphere of where we spend our money. So where are you spending the majority of your hard-earned dollars: department stores, the internet, home improvement stores? (Yes, there are female hardware enthusiasts who love hanging out at home improvement centers.)

_____

_____

_____

4. ***How Do You Spend (Cash, Credit, or Debit)?***

   Despite the fact that we have the convenience of the debit card to prevent us from using our credit cards and increasing our debt load, people are still out of control with swiping (debit *and* credit). Having the debit card has not helped, especially if you have no self-control. The biggest problem I see with people carrying the debit card is they forget that a bill has not been paid. They swipe because the money is available in their account. When they run out of money linked to the debit card, they start swiping the credit card. If self-control is an issue for you, neither method works. Carry cash and only use what you have allotted.

   _____

   _____

   _____

Walking through these questions will provide you a better understanding of your own behavior with money. If you truly have a big problem with shopping and that is the culprit to your spending, try these quick solutions and then seek professional help if you cannot get your spending under control. There are counselors and groups for shopaholics.

> ### *Solutions to Taming the Spending Beast within Us*
> - Understand your spending habits and the history of your spending.
> - Explore the reasons you love to shop.
> - Use a list and stick to it.
> - Always shop alone.
> - Bring the cash you have allotted to spend with you.
> - Only use credit cards you can pay off in full the following month.
> - Put credit cards out of reach or freeze them.
> - Keep tags on items and receipts in one place.

Several books examine the behavior of highly successful people or how the rich become rich. Depending on the article, you will get slightly different versions of the same thing. All of the books written on this subject lead back to one simple answer and solution: HABITS. People that reach the pinnacle of their success in building wealth create habits. These habits are repeated and stacked. If we examine the definition of habit, here is what we find: "practice" and "pattern." When we set our goals and put in place steps to achieve those goals, we have to practice them and turn them into a pattern. Then those habits become our behavior.

I've always wanted to live a debt-free life before I reached retirement. I envision my golden years traveling and spending time with my grandchildren. In my mind, stressing about money would be the last of my concerns. This is how it should be, don't you think? I saw my mother accomplish this, and although she never earned a lot of money, there was a peace of mind she exuded when she reached her retirement years. She sleeps well at night knowing she doesn't have to worry about a mortgage or looming credit card debt. "Stressing about money and debt can kill you," she said to me. Although I am several years from retirement, I am positive I will reach my goal of living mortgage and debt free.

Let's examine two habits that I set out to accomplish personally. One habit resulted in success, which led to a change in my mindset and behavior. The other was not so successful because I wasn't 100 percent committed to the habits that would lead to success.

I created the habit of paying myself first, no matter how much money I made. This means paying off my credit cards in full every month. This is an obsession, a rule, and a matter of course for myself. If I earn extra money, some of it goes into an account somewhere. Occasionally—but only occasionally—I treat myself. I examine my budget every month and make revisions when necessary. This habit is so engrained that I can't remember when it wasn't a habit. Because of these habits, my behavior concerning money has changed. I realized that the more I stuck to my habits, the more other natural traits were exhibited.

I believe we can do only three things with money: 1) save it, 2) spend it, or 3) give it away. I find it true that for those who are natural givers, they feel even better about giving when they have surplus money to give. Deep down inside I have the yearning to give by employing others. It feels good to pay someone for their work, to make someone feel their worth. My behavior with money would not have been possible if I hadn't created habits early in my life and if I didn't have someone reminding me the importance of this habit.

I have not been as successful with maintaining my weight because I simply never created the habits that were necessary for success. The vision isn't there—yet! I start and stop when it comes to exercise. Yes, I will admit this to my readers. My weight has been a struggle for me, and perhaps it's not so different from the struggle that many people have when it comes to their spending. It all comes back to creating the habits which will result in behavioral changes. I am successful in some areas of my life and not so successful in other areas. Think about it this way. Good habits will result in personal wins and successes and will also result in you becoming an expert. We like to take advice from people we view as successful in an area we want to succeed. We like what they have become. Who wouldn't take money advice from Mr. Warren Buffett? He has exemplified his wins. He created habits that would result in success.

Changing the Status Quo

The biggest mistake I see in a town like Atlanta—where image seems to be everything—is when people spend their last dollars to keep up appearances. I suppose this type of behavior has been going on since the beginning of time, but my lovely city has hit an all-time high in spending on looks.

People neglect saving for retirement to fund pre-kindergarten. The cost of some of these programs is mind-boggling. I had one client share that because of professional pressures, she should be able to afford an expensive school for her child. She was a young associate attorney who had not started making the big bucks in her profession. The title of her profession—much to her dismay—had nothing to do with the net cash flow coming into her household. What was really at stake was her image.

Do you keep up with the Joneses?

Parents will come up with so many excuses about why they need to empty out their banking accounts for the right school, when school is never the issue. Image is the issue. It is costing people a future filled with regret. Regret for not taking care of their retirement needs during their full potential earning years.

Titles are just titles. When I worked in corporate America, I had a coworker who had attended an Ivy League institution, and she carried on and bragged about her school. She went beyond school pride—which we all do—to the point of demeaning others who had not attended an Ivy League institution. All I could think about was the fact that she and I shared similar digits on our pay stubs, and I wasn't still paying off student loan debt. She was the poster child for the slogan, "You can't teach brains."

I am not an expert on human behavior. I don't have an explanation for why so many people feel the need to be relevant by spending beyond their means. The reasons are beyond the scope of this text. What I do know is keeping up with the Joneses will financially ruin you. Play in your own sandbox with your own plastic shovels. It's okay. You are not alone.

Net Worth Does Not Equal Cash Flow

Before we delve into calculating a person's net worth, I want to clear up a huge misconception many people have about the difference between having net worth and having cash flow. They are two completely different things. If you own something of value, it has net worth to you, but just because you have an asset that has value to you, it doesn't mean that it can create cash flow for you.

This is a huge mistake people make when they see others with material possessions or even items that have value. Many people who don't quite understand the concept of cash flow and net worth just make the assumption that *material possessions* means you are rolling in dough. Things are just things which don't always equate to liquid cash flow.

I will make a confession about a mistake I made that taught me a valuable lesson about sharing too much of my personal business with friends and relatives. I never thought people that I confided in would throw my words back at me to their advantage (boy, was I naive). I made the decision not to go on a group trip because my cash flow wasn't where I wanted it to be at the time. I was rebuilding my vacation account after depleting it from a trip I had taken to Europe that set me back a pretty penny. Needless to say, others were not happy that I made the decision not to take the trip. I told them regretfully but unapologetically that I couldn't spend the money. We all like taking trips, right? I have also made it a rule—and stuck with it—that certain funds are allocated for certain events. No exceptions. The first thing they brought up was what they assumed was my net worth, and because of the number they imagined to be my net worth, they believed I could afford the trip.

Wealth builders do not deplete or tap into rainy day funds or retirement money in order to take vacations. Many people do not understand this concept. Just because you have money sitting in a retirement account does not mean it furnishes your leisure or everyday cash flow needs. As a child, I often heard my mother say, "When you are saving for a purpose, pretend the money doesn't exist." That way of thinking is the mindset of a wealth builder. Wealth builders prepare themselves for rainy days and sleep soundly at night, knowing that money has been set aside for that very purpose. Other accounts are created for vacations and leisurely trips. That's why you set goals and set aside money for events.

But more importantly, you should feel okay saying no to spending money that you do not have or spending money that would require you to run up your credit card balance. As we age, we should feel comfortable saying no unapologetically without explanation.

Now, having disposable cash flow could lead to building a positive net worth. Denying your indulgences and paying down debt allows you to have extra money for a rainy day or add money to your investment account. Positive cash flow builds net worth, but only if you save the money rather than spend it just as fast as you receive it.

Calculating Your Net Worth and Facing It Head-on

Calculating your net worth is a simple math equation. Your assets (the things you own) minus your liabilities (the things you owe) equals your net worth. Your goal is to grow your net worth number, preferably with appreciating assets. Appreciating assets are those items in your financial house that have the potential to grow in value, like your 401(k) plan or the value of your real estate. What you don't want are your assets growing because you are accumulating too many personal assets and applying what I call a false sense of worth to the items. I see this when some women convince themselves that the handbag they purchased could be a collector's item one day. Let's face it, even though our personal wardrobes may have cost us several thousand dollars, they don't grow in value. You will likely receive far less than what you paid if you tried to sell it.

ASSETS - LIABILITIES = NET WORTH

Now I want you to sit down and calculate this number. I have provided a worksheet in the appendix that will help you calculate your net worth. Plug in items such as the worth of your savings/checking accounts, real estate values, investment accounts, retirement accounts, business asset value, cash value of your life insurance policy, etc. Add up these numbers and subtract from the total your student loan debt, credit card balances, car loans, mortgage balance, and all other revolving and installment debt. This exercise will allow you to face your net worth. Do not be surprised if this number is negative! You would be surprised by the number of professionals who have a negative net worth. Our goal is to turn this number into something positive and you have the power and possess the behavior to do so. Facing what is written on paper is the first step.

The second step is to ask yourself how you got here. Do you have a negative or low net worth because you took out a student loan to further your education? If this is the case, do not beat yourself up. Simply make sure you stay on top of the payments because that's one loan that will stay with you for life if you allow it to. Student loans cannot be written off in a bankruptcy. I have encountered individuals who used schooling as a procrastination technique because they weren't quite sure what they wanted to do with their life, so they became lifelong students and picked up student loans along the way. This is a bad idea. Never waste money on student loans while you are "finding yourself." There are far cheaper ways to get in tune with your inner spirit or your yearning to become a _____ (you fill in the blank).

Needless to say, growing your net worth is the start to building wealth, even if wealth is defined so differently from person to person. When you look at the net worth that you have calculated on the worksheet, how does it make you feel? Does your number reflect your idea of wealth? If the number is negative, then you have work to do. But that's okay because by now you have identified where the leak in your financial growth is. Our goal is to create a woman of wealth. Wealth that has substance and not wealth created with *stuff*.

Growing up I often heard my mother say to my dad that she wanted to have "something." When I was a child, I never knew what she meant. That something in my mind meant material possessions. As I've grown older and worked closely in helping my mother with her finances, I now know that "something" meant a legacy for her children. She wanted to create generational wealth which was something she could leave behind for her children. That wealth wasn't just monetary but a wealth filled with great savings habits and financial knowledge. My mother always felt that even if a woman was married and had a husband, she should always make sure she created her own little private emergency fund, "Just in case." "Just in case" encompasses an array of pitfalls that can happen when you are married and raising a family. I took her words of advice and never forgot. I have always saved for that rainy day.

NOTES

Chapter 3
Creating Your Spending Plan (The Budget)

What Are Your Financial Goals?

THE WORD "BUDGET" MAKES PEOPLE CRINGE. THINKING ABOUT PUTTING one in place can seem like a daunting task. We always work backward when we do finally get the nerve to create one. The first mistake we make when we create a budget is that we save after we've paid everything else. What's wrong with putting your personal financial goals ahead of others such as creditors? Absolutely nothing! This is how it should be, yet we reverse the process. Define your financial goals and then build a budget around them. The best time to start this as an adult is when you land your first job.

Many young professionals go out and buy a car and find a place to live before they even think about saving a penny. Bad idea! Granted, everything depends on your circumstances, but if you are in a situation that would allow you to live rent free or have very few expenses when you land your first job out of college, this is surely the ideal situation that will give you a chance to think about what you want your life to look like in the future.

When I graduated from college, I went back home, and my mother told me to grab a bill because she was not up for me living rent free as an adult. Tough love and rightly expected. When I did start looking for an apartment, I created a living budget—a spending plan—around what I wanted to save and spend on living expenses. That meant that

I would purchase a less expensive car and spend even less on an apartment if it meant that I could put something away in savings. That has always been a priority.

I have a client who I so admire. She has really taken the necessary steps it takes to build wealth and live a fruitful, exciting retirement if she ever retires. During her medical residency program, she heard me give a presentation on wealth building. When she landed her first job out of residency, she came to see me to put a plan in place before going out and making her first big ticket purchases—her first luxury car! We examined what the car would cost and how her household would look if she made the purchase, how long she wanted to finance the car, and what the final cost would be. This was a big step for someone who was still driving her first car from college. Needless to say, we walked through the plan of buying the car and all of the costs associated with the purchase. She has taken this approach with all of her purchases, still taking into consideration her financial goals and what she wanted her future to look like.

So many people wait until they get into trouble before they ask for help or begin to create a plan. Don't let this be you! Take some time out of your busy schedule and sit, *really* sit, in silence and imagine the life you want to live now and in retirement, even if retirement has never been a goal. As the great Steven Covey has said, "Begin with the end in mind." Think about your immediate short-term goals and then go big! What does the end look like in mind? I personally believe that our thoughts order our steps in life.

Now ask yourself the following questions:
1. What does my financial picture look like now?
2. How would I like for my finances to look in the future?
3. Am I living paycheck to paycheck?

(cont.)

4. Is there money left over at the end of each pay period? If there is, what am I doing with the money? Does it just sit in my checking account and disappear?

5. If there isn't any money left over after getting paid, what can I do to generate more income?

6. Do I have the time to generate more money if I have to? What skills do I have that would help me generate more money?

7. How do I envision my financial future? What do I plan on doing about it right now?

Not only do you need to meditate on these questions, but write out your answers to these questions and then begin to take the necessary steps to change your future. Here's the most revealing part about all of this: once you write out your answers to these questions, read your responses out loud. Hear yourself say what you have been thinking. Speak your goals into existence. Talk about an eye-opening experience. You might be surprised what you discover.

I worked for a Fortune 500 company for sixteen years, and toward the end of my career at this company, I really started hating my job. Don't get me wrong, I was very grateful for the opportunity the job provided for me. I learned a great deal during my years of employment, but toward the end, I was dissatisfied. Something was missing, and I truly had a void in my life as far as my career was concerned. I was still performing well but wasn't very happy getting out of bed going to the job—yes, *job*, not *career*—every day. The company started going through downsizing and this process took place over a three-year period. Every time the company would make an announcement about the next pool of layoffs, I thought to myself, *I really would like to be one of the lucky ones who get downsized*. The company went through a couple of rounds over a course of three years, and I never got "lucky." I thought for years of quitting but didn't have the courage to walk away. I had the golden handcuffs clasped around my wrist, and I simply could not walk away. I was used to the perks of the company, and I thought they were enough to keep me happy. At least that's what I told myself time and time again. I would say, "I am lucky because so many people would love to have this job." Company car, corporate credit card and a great 401(k) plan. What more could a person want out of life? I could have hung around until I retired and lived a very nice life. But I was miserable. I honestly felt like I was not using my brain cells!

At the end of 2008, the company announced that they were going to go through another round of layoffs at the beginning of 2009. This time I said out loud, "I hope I get laid off this time." I caught myself when I said this. My heart started pounding because I had actually never said this out loud. After several rounds, I felt like my time had come and this would be it, even though I was at the top of my game. I was one of the top sales people in my region, but I felt like something was different this time. Just like a woman who starts the nesting effect right before the baby comes, I started the same thing anticipating that my dismissal would finally come. I was going to be released from the golden handcuffs that had me shackled for so long. The rest of my life would begin. My rebirth was finally coming! That was my prayer.

I went out and purchased my own car because I had driven a company car for so long. I made sure all of my bills were caught up and all credit cards had been paid off. I checked my accounts to make sure I was going to be okay financially just in case I had spoken the layoff into existence. I really gave serious thought to how I wanted to spend the rest of my life. Delivering medical samples to physicians was definitely out of the question, despite being paid well to do it. I wanted to spend the rest of my life helping people manage their finances and get their financial houses in order. Deep down inside, this had always been my destiny. I majored in finance in college and minored in banking. At the age of eighteen, I told myself that I wanted to work on Wall Street and trade stocks. I was offered a job out of college at a brokerage firm but didn't accept the position because I felt the salary was too low. Instead, I accepted a position at a banking institution.

In January 2009, I received a call that changed the course of the rest of my life. I was told that I would be part of the next group who would be downsized. I had the opportunity to apply for other positions inside of the company if I wanted to. I knew that if I didn't leave then, I would never get the courage to do so on my own, so I took the severance package.

I truly feel like I created my destiny by speaking it into existence. I got what I wanted. I think God created a situation that would allow me to have the strength and courage to walk away. I have to admit, though, that my ego was bruised. Even though I wished to be a part of the process, I was still in disbelief that it happened to a top performer. That's business, I suppose. What I learned from it all was that anyone is disposable when she works for someone else. Your job is never secure.

The downsizing gave me time to think about my future. How would my future change? What did I want to do with the rest of my life now that I had a world of options? What adjustments did I need to make with my personal finances? After I said out loud that I wanted to become a financial advisor, the next thing I did was look at my budget. I sliced and diced my spending and went through the exercise of determining what I could live with and what could be eliminated from my life. I calculated how much money I had on hand and how long it would last me through the transition to pursue my purpose. I knew I had something to give back when I realized that I had a few years of reserve money that allowed me to create a career helping others with their finances. I didn't want another job that paid well but didn't fulfill my soul. Walking in purpose and on purpose is priceless and no price tag can be placed on it.

Mistakes We Make Creating a Budget

The first and obvious mistake we make in creating a budget is we simply do not create one. I am amazed at the number of people who have expressed their desire to purchase a big ticket item like a car or a house, yet they have no clue what their disposable income looks like (the money left over after you have paid all bills). They do not work with a budget, so a simple answer like disposable income doesn't come easy. Start with pen and paper before you transfer your numbers to whatever software you use. There's something about writing with pen and paper that resonate in our brain and stimulates our brain cells!

We think short term. Reviewing your monthly budget allows you to think about upcoming events. If something is on the horizon, this is the time to reorganize other line items and add a line item for upcoming events. I keep a line item in my budget labeled "Membership" to cover fees in the various organizations I am involved in. One of the organizations assessed its members a one-time fee that would be due six months out. Granted six months is short term, but I had to make immediate adjustments to my budget to cover the assessment. I moved money from my personal spending allowance and temporarily added more to the membership line item. When the six months rolled around to pay the assessment, I had the money put away and ready to cut a check for the fee. That was a personal example, but you can apply this same strategy to anything that is long term, making sure it has a place in your budget, such as line items for a down payment on a house or car.

We are unrealistic. Giving yourself a fifty-dollar-per-month allowance to cover all personal items such as coffee runs and snacks is completely unrealistic, especially if you are accustomed to spending freely on these types of items. I would suggest if you have never completed a budget before in your life, take a month and record all of your spending or review your bank statement. The important thing is creating realistic line items that you can stick with and not fall off of the budget bandwagon after one month because you went over your budget.

We spend more than we earn. This is the whole purpose of the budget. You are trying to stay on track. Unfortunately, when the budget is too strict and unrealistic, people go back to their old habits and go over the budget by spending more than what was allotted for in the line items. Try to stick to it, and if you fall off of the budget wagon, just get back up and start again the following month. Don't beat yourself up. It is possible to do!

We keep an overly elaborate budget. I see this one quite frequently. Spreadsheets highlighted with colors and pie charts all stored in a folder on the computer. We have advanced to using all of the fancy technology and apps. It's not that complicated. Make sure you can put your hands on your budget. If you like all of the fancy apps, print out a copy of your budget to stick in your purse or fold up and place in your wallet. This allows you to go back and revisit the budget with ease rather than waiting for your phone to get in a good range so you can log in to see your budget. Pulling out a slip of paper is so much faster! You can write a note on your budget if you suddenly remember something that needs to be added for next month, like the dance recital costume fees for your daughter (actual line item in one of my monthly budgets).

We allow our checking account balance to get too low. This point is for those who are completely paperless (most people nowadays) who create a budget based on what is in the checking account. Set a cushion in your account and never allow your account to go below it. This never fails. There will be a time when you forget something that should have cleared your account or forget that something has to be paid. Technology does fail. I have seen paychecks deposit late and overdrafts occur because people had their bills set up to pay out automatically. Keeping a cushion for fluke incidents never hurts and could save you from an embarrassing and costly mistake.

We never adjust the budget. Once you make it part of your life, a budget can be your constant sidekick or the little voice that reminds you of your goals and what you can and can't spend. Some people create a budget at the beginning of the year when they set their New Year's Resolutions to get their finances in order and never revisit it again until the following year. Get in the habit of looking at your budget at least once a month. That may sound extreme, but when you are trying to make financial changes in your life, this is necessary. What you planned for in January will not be the same in July. We all have adjustments in our lives that require our attention. Nothing stays the same from January through December and neither should your budget.

We never create a rainy day fund. I saved the best for last. Until your rainy day fund is filled, having a line item in your budget for this account is a must. Something will happen and you must be prepared to handle it head-on. You can start the account with bonus money — tax refunds, monetary gifts, end-of-year bonuses, etc. — that may be coming your way. Continue to fill it monthly until you reach your goal.

Zero Is the Magic Number

Having nothing left over when you create your budget is a good thing. Every penny should have a home. As strange as this may sound, sometimes this concept seems difficult for people to grasp. Starting out with your net take-home pay and ending with the magic number zero should be your goal.

Let me elaborate on what I mean by zero being the magic number. Every item that you spend a penny on should be accounted for, unless you are using cash for spending to cover your everyday expenses. I do believe that you spend less when you use cash. Once the cash is gone, you cannot go back and reach into the cookie jar of your checking account. Some people find this method more regimented, but if you are trying to graduate to another level with your spending, then trying new methods does not hurt until you find out what works best for you.

I have created a list of common expense items in the appendix of the book to help you create your expense list and capture as many items as possible. If you have a difficult time with budgeting and you use expense money for "fun money," then you should go ahead and take that money out of your account and live on cash until you have become comfortable with managing money. "Know thyself" is so important when creating a realistic budget. If spending is truly a weakness of yours, at this point you may want to rely on software, like that found on mint.com, to help you sort expenses and money used for pleasure.

Items like fuel for the car may be difficult to use cash for. This may be a good place to use your credit card if you do not want to go inside of the convenience store to pay for fuel. I would not use a debit card to pay for fuel at the pump. I have heard personal accounts of people having their identity stolen by using debit cards at the pump. Use a fuel card or credit card and make sure the cards are paid in full each month out of your fuel allowance. Do not buy potato chips or snacks with your fuel card. Don't fall into this easy trap. You may find that you cannot pay the card in full one month and end up paying finance charges on a bag of potato chips. The card should simply be used for one purpose: the convenience of paying at the pump when you have placed yourself on a cash diet.

Here's my personal confession about how I use credit and debit cards. I do not use any software to help with my budget every month. I like writing my budget down on a piece of paper and carrying it with me everywhere I go. I like having it readily accessible. I use my credit card to make all of my purchases so that I have a nice record of my expenditures at the end of the year to see which categories I spend the most money on. I record my credit card transactions in an old fashion check register just as I would with any debit card transactions. I use a pencil to record the transactions, and I pay the card off in full each month. Why the pencil, you might ask? The pencil isn't permanent, and it allows me to see what hasn't been officially paid in my register. Once I pay the item, I go over it in permanent ink, indicating that it has been paid. We all need to find a method that works best for us. Writing out my balances keeps me on my toes when it comes to my finances. I do understand that this method may be far too antiquated for people that love using apps for everything. Here are my thoughts on that particular point. Technology has not gotten us any closer to reducing the amount of credit card debt in this country!

Your Checking Account: A Ray of Sunshine

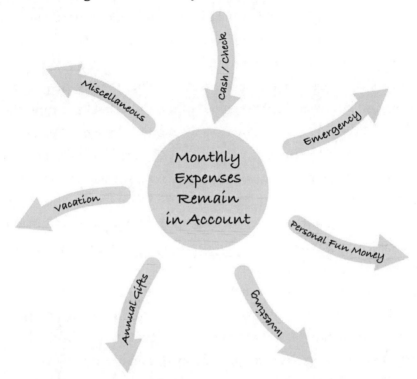

Your checking account should act as a conduit to fund everything in your life and all of your financial goals. Your spending money and monthly expenses should be the only money that remains in that account. Just imagine the sun acting as your account.

Your paycheck goes into the account and rays from the sun shoot out of the account. Each sun ray has its own special name: Rainy Day Fund, Vacation, Annual Dues and Memberships, Down Payment on Car, Auto Maintenance, Investments, etc. I like a two-day window on money sitting in the account that will be used to fund other areas just mentioned. If the money sits in the account too long, you are going to find something else to spend it on. Something will come up that will seem far more important than saving for a rainy day. You will say, "Well, today is a rainy day and I need the money." Make sure all of your sun rays are set on automatic debit. As an example, if you are paid on the fifteenth of every month, set your automatic investments on the seventeenth. If the fifteenth falls on a weekend, most companies will pay you the Friday before, so you will not incur an overdraft if the money comes out two days later.

You never miss what you don't have. This is why people who automatically have money taken out of their paychecks to fund their retirement accounts never really miss the money. Trust me. People who don't do this will not have any money saved away for retirement. We must treat our everyday goals the same way we would if we were investing for retirement. Automatic contributions can be your friend. Please do not get automatic contributions for savings goals mixed up with automatic payment for credit cards. That is something you want to keep under your control in the event you just don't have the money to pay the credit card company at the moment.

Besides savings and investing—which are rays of sunshine because they truly will make you feel good when your goals are reached with little effort—very little should be placed on automatic debit from your checking account. You should have control over the times and dates your own money is moving in and out of your account. Never set up automatic drafts to gym memberships or credit card companies. If times get rough, you want wiggle room. You don't want anyone else having access to your money. The only other exceptions I make to this rule are mortgage payments, car notes, student loans, and insurance payments (life and automobile). Having the roof over your head paid for and transportation costs covered is always a priority. You also don't want the car insurance to lapse because you forgot to pay it and then get into an accident. Tragedy never makes an appointment with you so always protect yourself in times of uncertainty.

NOTES

Chapter 4

What's in Your Money Buckets?

THE MONEY BUCKETS REPRESENT THE IMPORTANCE OF BUILDING A diversified portfolio of assets to allow for multiple places to pull from during your lifetime and in retirement. What will not be discussed is the order and strategy by which you should pull from these buckets because we simply cannot predict the future. Every personal situation is different, but I will share with you the multiple buckets I have created for myself. Some of the items in my buckets are not available to everyone because, as I have stated, times change.

For those who have the desire to build wealth, you need to think about your money differently and realize that it cannot manage itself. It needs attention and needs to be nurtured just like you would if you were trying to grow anything. You cannot set it and forget it. That may come as a disappointment to some, but for those who have created wealth, they paid attention to what was going on with their money.

I personally feel that we are simply living in a different time compared to years past. The financial markets are extremely volatile. Fundamental strategies that were once the saving grace of the long-term investors have suddenly ceased to exist. With every newsflash, you see an extremely different shift in the stock market. With the slightest hint of a rate hike by the Federal Reserve, the market numbers turn red. Don't get me wrong. I believe in the stock market. Gains I have made in the stock market afforded me the opportunity to walk away from my traditional nine-to-five job and fund a small business. Gains on stocks afforded my husband and me the opportunity to place a sizable down payment on our home which will now be paid off well before retirement. Even with all of the great things I have been able to do because of money in the market, I am smart enough to know that the stock market isn't the answer to all of your financial growth needs. Some may argue differently, but the majority will not.

So my buckets do not represent withdrawal strategies for retirement. They do show the diversity of funds you should carry in your portfolios to weather the many storms you might see during your lifetime.

Working closely with your personal advisor is the best strategy for determining the percentages you need in each bucket and the timing of your withdrawals from them. I simply want to stress the importance of diversification for those who want to build wealth beyond simply having money sitting in your institutional checking or saving accounts.

I will share with you the types of items I have placed in my personal money buckets. Based on my income, I have surpassed what some experts say you will need in retirement based on your current income today. Think about that. Personally speaking, quantifying a specific number creates some peace of mind, but I do realize that there are no guarantees or certainties to our future except death. There are clients who feel comfortable knowing that if they reach "X" amount of dollars, they will be happy and comfortable in retirement. My life so far has been anything but predictable, so I have not defined my specific number. I wonder if people like Warren Buffet, Bill Gates, or Oprah Winfrey—my personal "shero"—defined their "X" or whether they kept creating and continued to build on their successes because they were doing what they loved to do.

What have I personally done to build wealth? Every time my income has increased, the contributions to one of my buckets have increased. I've never taken money from my retirement account, even when the market tumbled in 2008. I did, however, have plenty of time on my side for recovery. I set certain financial milestone goals for things I wanted to do that would cost money, like family vacations, buying a car with short-term financing, or paying off my mortgage before hitting retirement. All of these goals required me to make certain sacrifices and choices with my money. Saving for these goals meant not spending in other areas.

I personally don't know what enough money looks like because I am sure I can find a way to spend it all even if that means giving it away. What I do know for certain is we need cash flow sources throughout our lifetime. This is especially important during your working years because your money can continue to grow through compounding interest. I believe if we nurture and fill our buckets, along with implementing modified behavioral changes, our buckets will be enough to take care of our needs for the rest of our lifetime.

I feel very fortunate to have had the opportunity to start filling my money buckets early in my career. When I graduated from college, I had very little student loan debt. As a matter of fact, I only owed around $1,700 when I came out of college. I am sure someone screamed after reading this number, considering the mounting student loan debt students carry today. I was able to get through college on savings from working summer jobs since the age of sixteen, Social Security payments after my father's death, working on campus my entire four years in college, and other forms of financial aid. Because there were very few family funds available to contribute to my education, I qualified for all of the available financial aid provided for students in need. These funds became available once I depleted the cash I had saved for college my freshman year. This was another lesson I learned about financial aid as a young eighteen-year-old entering college. Your available funds carry more weight than your parents' when you are applying for financial aid.

Because I always knew I wanted to go to college, my mother told me early on that I needed to save money from my summer jobs to cover my college costs. Knowing that I would have to foot the bill for college, I thought long and hard about my choices. I knew I needed to attend a school that I could afford to pay out of pocket if I had to take on part-time work while in school.

During my senior year in high school, my mother gave me the checks from Social Security to save on my own. She told me she didn't care what I did with the money but that I better make a wise decision and save for college if I wanted to attend. Which I did! By the time I was eighteen and ready to head off to school, I had saved about eight thousand dollars. That was enough to get me through my freshman year. After my freshman year, when all of my money was depleted, financial aid kicked in and covered the rest of my education, along with the money I earned from work study.

I do feel a sense of duty to share my knowledge with society because society took care of me when I needed it most. Having virtually no debt coming out of school meant that I had a head start over my peers in terms of saving and working on my behavior with money.

Short-Term Bucket

I personally think this is the most important bucket because it holds all of our emergency and short-term needs without costing us penalties if we have to tap into it. The short-term bucket consists of financial assets that we keep on hand in a liquid form which are readily available for our immediate needs. These liquid assets should not lose value when we try to retrieve them for our financial needs, unlike selling a piece of stock, mutual fund or selling a piece of real estate.

Formal rules of thumb dictate that we keep three months of living expenses on hand if there are two consistent income earners in one household and six months' worth of living expenses if there is one income earner or one source of funds coming into the household.

If we are experiencing a tough economy, it might take you longer than three to six months to find employment in the event of a job loss. During the recession that began in late 2007 and early 2008, several people experienced horrific bouts of unemployment that lasted in many cases well over two years. Individuals and households depleted their savings, and unemployment insurance wasn't enough to make ends meet. For those who eventually found work, they were often underemployed, which meant that they were still not making enough to cover their living expenses.

If you have a specialized skill that is not transferable to another job, you might want to keep more cash on hand (or begin to seek job training for a wider set of skills in the meantime). Finally, if you are an entrepreneur, you may even want to keep twelve months of cash on hand. Some argue that twelve months' worth of cash is a lost opportunity cost when the money can be working elsewhere, but as you can see, the amount you keep will depend on your individual situation.

I have learned you cannot argue with preventing someone from getting a good night's rest! I have worked with several single female professionals who just don't sleep well if they do not keep a certain amount of cash on hand, and I personally will not argue the point with them, especially if they have experienced losses in the past. I will, however, warn them that they can reach a point of diminishing returns because they have too much cash sitting in an account not working its compound interest magic due to extremely low interest rates. At this point, you need to consider getting out of your comfort zone and have a conversation with your advisor.

In my personal short-term liquid cash bucket, I have a combination of various liquid instruments that includes a savings account, a money market account, Series I bonds, and cash value in my whole life insurance policies. All of these are different forms of cash that are readily available when needed but pay different forms of interest.

Additionally, I also have several small accounts (rays of sunshine) that are liquid. These are for goals that I have set for myself or upcoming expenses that I may have to pay. Examples of small goal accounts might include vacation, memberships (civic organization dues), and buying a vehicle, just to name a few. Having multiple accounts is a style preference for some advisors because I have had colleagues say that they tell their clients to lump all of their miscellaneous money in one account and draw from it when they are ready to go on vacation or buy themselves a car. I argue that we are visual creatures. If you lump all of the money in one big account, you might forget what has been allocated for the car or vacation. Keeping separately named accounts allows you to keep track of your progress.

There are several banking institutions that will allow you to create one customer account and allow several named accounts under your customer number. My favorite is CapitalOne360 (www.capitalone360.com). This is not an endorsement for CapitalOne, but I found the setup process at this institution to be rather easy. The purpose of these small accounts is not long term, so you shouldn't expect to gain large returns at the expense of your principle.

For those who are starting to build wealth, I want you to notice the various types of short-term instruments available for your short-term bucket. You should also be aware that although these instruments pay varying interest rates, you will still have to pay the taxes on the interest gained from them. There will be no interest to pay on the cash value in your life insurance policy because usually the cash value is a return of the premium.[13] Details about how cash value in life insurance works is beyond the scope of this text. This may be a good time to make a note to yourself and research the advantages of owning whole life insurance as part of your overall wealth building strategy.

Most people have something in their short-term bucket. As a matter of fact, you will usually see the short term and long-term bucket, which I will cover shortly, with some value tied to it. We should start thinking about the options that are available for all of the buckets in our quest to build wealth. Filling your short-term bucket should be your first goal. Think beyond the traditional checking or savings account for your liquid short-term bucket. Every little bit of interest counts and gets us closer to reaching our financial goals. Compounding over a long period of time is our friend, even in a low interest environment.

---

[13] Whole life insurance policies contain an important savings element known as cash value. The cash value depends upon the type of product, the face amount, the time in force, and the amount of premium payments.

SHORT-TERM BUCKET EXAMPLES

Cash

Treasury Bills

Money Market

Cash Value Life Insurance

Certificates of Deposits < 12 months

Series I Bonds

Midterm Bucket

While I think the short-term bucket is the most important for our everyday needs, the midterm bucket is my favorite bucket because it provides flexibility and a wider range of items that can be placed in the bucket. This bucket can also be the riskiest of the four buckets we will discuss because you don't have to wait until retirement to take money out of this one. You could encounter more short-term losses if you are not patient. You can take on as much or as little risk as you like in this bucket. Despite the risk of investing, this bucket can make you rich with time and patience. This will be the only place in this book I use the word "rich." The word "rich" is relative, but here's what I mean. You must invest consistently, even in volatile markets. It's one of the simplest ways to build wealth, yet hardly anyone ever does it. The average novice investor buys into the market when it is up because they hear that the market is hot, and they pull out of the market when it is down because they panic. During volatile markets like we often experience, dollar cost averaging is your friend. Dollar cost averaging is a technique of automatically investing the same amount of money on a consistent basis regardless of the market trends. Because you can buy more shares, whether it is a stock or a mutual fund, during a flat or volatile market rather than one that is rising, you get more bang for your buck (more for your money).

Because many people have very little knowledge of the possibilities for the midterm, this bucket is often filled with nothing, one big goose egg. We know that it's important to put money away to save for a rainy day (even though most people don't have enough in their rainy day/emergency fund). Saving for the short term is often easy because you simply open up a savings account and add cash to the account. We even know that it's important to save for retirement, so we rely on our employers to make the first step for us in this area by offering a 401(k) plan or something similar. Like robots, we contribute a percentage of our income by throwing a dart at one of the selections, or we ask a coworker. What we don't know how to do is build wealth in between the short-term and long-term buckets.

Building wealth in the middle bucket requires work on your part. You must teach yourself or you must seek help from an advisor. Most people will not go through the trouble to learn what they can do so the midterm bucket goes unfilled most of the time. From what I've seen, people's neglect of the midterm bucket is common regardless of income levels. It is a matter of financial knowledge whether this bucket is filled or remains empty throughout our lifetime. We simply do not know or we were never taught other ways to save and build wealth. We fear the unknown. The media does not help either when we see or hear the announcement of the gains and losses of the market every day.

Even though it is labeled the midterm bucket, you want to start filling this bucket last after other important matters have been taken care of. More important matters might be building your emergency fund or taking advantage of a free company match from your employer's 401(k) or retirement plan.

When I graduated from college and started working for First Atlanta Bank, I purchased my first subscriptions to the magazines *Kiplinger's Personal Finance* and *Money*. *Money* gives the rundown on all of the mutual fund families and previews their returns in the back of the magazine. *Kiplinger's* provides great consumer advice on various topics. The information from these magazines was great for a young professional woman living on her own. I read all about the various mutual fund families available to invest in (provided you met the minimum balance). Besides, from reading about them in a college textbook and seeing them on statements from customers, I didn't know anyone who owned mutual funds.

My mother came from an era of high-interest-rate CDs and that was the only investment vehicle I heard about growing up. Mutual funds were new to me and pretty exciting to learn about as a twenty-two-year-old college graduate.

After I made my first stock purchase—a few shares in a home improve-ment store chain—I set my eyes on putting money in a mutual fund. I encountered a problem, though. I needed to save five thousand dollars to place in the mutual fund. This was my first life lesson in the differences between stocks and mutual funds. Mutual funds sometimes require a minimum to open an account, and you cannot trade them throughout the day (intraday) like a stock. Mutual funds are bought and sold at the close of the business day. The minimum required lump sum to open the mutual fund account served as a road block for my investing, so I continued to buy shares of various stocks when I had the cash.

What I didn't know at the time was I was starting to fill my midterm bucket of money. After following a coworker's stock tips—which caused me to lose quite a bit of my money—I sold all of the stocks I had in my brokerage account at the time and only made future stock purchases when I was familiar with the company and did all of my own research. I was a novice investor at the time and definitely needed to lower my risk by being in mutual funds.

You can always buy a share of stock in an open market. Besides the trading fee, which is fairly low with most brokerage houses, the only fee involved in stock trading is the price of the stock itself, which varies from company to company. Mutual funds, however, are just that, a fund of various financial instruments that can only be bought based on the closing day's price.

Mutual funds and stocks can be great financial instruments to place in your midterm bucket. You have the opportunity to increase your return potential in this bucket based on your risk tolerance. You can take the money out when you want or let it ride. Mutual fund fees come in two categories: ongoing yearly fees (expense ratio) and transaction fees (loads) paid when you buy or sell shares in a fund. Depending on the mutual funds you own, you will also have to pay long- or short-term capital gains taxes on the money, even if you do not take it out. You do, however, have fewer risks compared to a share of stock because a mutual fund is basically bundling several instruments which softens the blow if one goes down in price and the other goes up in price. With mutual funds, you can create a neutral loss effect if one of the companies in the fund goes up in price and the other goes down in price. That's why small investors often stick to mutual funds. If you own one share of stock and the price drops, you lose, and there is nothing else that can soften the blow of lost money. But there is an advantage to owning the stock. If the price goes up, you will not have to pay gains on the stock until it is sold.

Another favorite mid-term bucket asset that has gained popularity over the years is the ETF (Exchange Traded Funds). The simplest way to understand an ETF is to look at it like a mutual fund that can be traded throughout the day like a stock. The expense ratios on ETFs are low and the investor can trade an entire index with ease and simplicity. Each trade costs a fee, just like trading a share of stock. You can learn more about ETFs and all of the fund families who carry them by doing your internet homework if you care to get into this market.

The mid-term bucket is ideal for any financial instrument that has better return potential than the short-term bucket, which means that there are quite a few options. If you are holding mutual funds, ETFs, or stocks in this bucket, you should set a time limit on when you take the money out. You want to make sure you hold the instruments longer than a year (one year and a day will work). Otherwise you may encounter short-term capital gains rates. Short-term capital gains rates do not benefit from any special tax treatment. You pay your regular ordinary income tax rates on stocks and mutual funds held for less than one year and a day. For stocks and mutual funds held longer than one year, you benefit from long-term capital gains rates, which will vary from 0, 15 or 20 percent for most tax payers. Just remember, you can take the money out when you want, and the tax you pay on your gains will depend on the time you take them out and your tax bracket. It's a good idea to chat with your tax advisor if you have tax questions related to your specific situation.

MIDTERM BUCKET EXAMPLES

STOCKS

MUTUAL FUNDS

CDs WITH MATURITIES > 1 YR

ETF (Exchange Traded Funds)

BONDS WITH MATURITIES > 1 YR

Long-Term Bucket

I would venture to say that most people who work for a company that offers a retirement plan have something in their long-term bucket. According to the *American's Benefit Council 401(k) Fast Facts,* updated April 2014, "Nearly 80 percent of full-time workers have access to employer-sponsored retirement plans and more than 80 percent of these workers participate in the plans."

When opportunity with little effort presents itself to us, we take it. The unfortunate part about this fact is when we are presented with the opportunity to invest in the retirement plan, most Americans play roulette when it comes to making a selection of the offerings. We consult with our colleagues and find out how they are investing for retirement or we take the very safe road and undertake very little risk for our time horizon.

I have met with many clients who did not know what the company match was on their 401(k) plan. If you don't know what the company match is on your plan, find out. Never walk away from free money! The match is decadent icing on a cake. If you are in a position to make a contribution to the sponsored plan, make sure you are contributing up to at least the company match. Free money compounded over several working years adds up to a nice nest egg.

What is usually in the long-term bucket? Employer-sponsored retirement plans, IRAs, Roth IRAs, Deferred Compensation Plans, and real estate are all examples of financial assets that can fund your long-term bucket. The premise behind the long-term bucket is saving for retirement. You want to make sure you have time on your side with this bucket. If you decide to take the smart route and start funding this bucket at an early age (before thirty) your risk tolerance can be different compared to your midterm bucket, which you want access to before retirement.

In most situations, if you take money out of your long-term bucket before you reach 59.5 years old, you will be penalized for early with-drawal. This bucket is meant to fund retirement or your long-term goals that you are not in a rush to reach. But it's best to start early!

I am sure the one thing that stands out on this list of long-term bucket examples is real estate. I will first state that I am currently not a realtor. I do, however, believe that owning real estate can be a great means to help fund your cash flow during retirement. I will reiterate "owning" real estate can be a great means to help with cash flow during retirement. This is where my opinion might differ from someone who considers themselves a real estate expert. If you own real estate outright, you have less stress on your hands and can sleep better at night knowing the mortgage on your property is free and clear. I have heard frustrating stories from clients who own rental property and have had a headache trying to collect rents from the tenant who happens to be habitually late with rent payments. The owners end up having to cover the mortgage payment on the property out of their pockets before the rent is collected. This is not how the real estate ownership game should be played.

If I looked at the rate of return on my personal residence over the past seventeen years that I have owned the property, my ROI (return on investment) would be negative if you factored in all of the costs associated with owning the property (principle, interest, taxes, insurance, maintenance, and improvements). This would probably be true for most people who have owned real estate over a long period. Yes, I would have a gain if I sold it based on what it is worth minus what I owe, but my overall return would be negative. The average investor never factors in all of the costs associated with acquiring real estate. Now, once I pay this baby off, it would make for great rental property. In essence, I would be paying myself back for all of the years I have covered the cost to live on the property. The cash flow is what is important and not the rate of return I receive on the property. This is what most people who accumulate residential real estate as an investment think about—the cash flow.

Because of the potential cash flow advantages of owning real estate and the fact that it cannot be easily liquidated if you need cash in a hurry, it has the honor of being placed in the long-term bucket category, but I make the distinction of labeling real estate as a long-term *asset* verses a long-term *investment*. This is why your portfolio or buckets should be diversified. There is no immediate return on real estate unless you're getting it at a steal and can flip it. Most people do not fall in the "flipping expert" category because flipping properties takes great knowledge and skills.

The ideal way to own real estate, in my opinion, is to own the property outright and use the rents that come in on the property as one of the means to fund your cash flow during retirement. If, however, your goal is to build an inventory of rental properties, you can also use the rental payments to pay off the mortgage of another property. Another strategy, depending on the size of the payment, is to divide the rental check into three piles: retirement cash flow, payment on the rent of another property, and cushion money to cover expenses on your rental property. The latter pile should really be a priority if you do not have funds set aside to cover rental maintenance costs.

There are several seminars and books that delve into the techniques of owning real estate. Unless you are flipping the property, real estate is truly a long-term asset and falls into your long-term bucket. Owning real estate is also a great way to leave an inheritance. I spent a little more time covering real estate because I get frequent questions on how real estate fits with the rest of the financial wealth building picture.

One of my favorite long-term bucket fillers is the Roth IRA. So, if you qualify for the Roth IRA, you may want to consider investing in one while you have the chance. Contributions to the Roth IRA, unlike the traditional IRA, are restricted by income. There is no need for me to give you the income numbers because they can change annually. Your best bet is to go to the IRS website or do an internet search for the current Roth IRA income limits. Depending on your income, you can make a full or partial nondeductible contribution (nondeductible means you cannot deduct on your income tax return). Everyone who has earned income can contribute to a Traditional IRA (unlike the Roth IRA), but the contributions may or may not be deductible. Your

CPA or tax preparer should be able to determine whether you qualify for the contribution.

One benefit of the Roth IRA compared to the traditional IRA is you do not have to pay taxes on the gains that have accumulated in the account over the years. You are also not required to pull money out of the account when you reach 70.5 years old. Some investors find it beneficial to own both a Roth IRA and traditional IRA. You can use funds from the Roth IRA to cover taxes on the gains from the traditional IRA or any tax deferred account you have created.

Additionally, do research on the types of employer sponsored retirement plans that don't fall under pension plans that allow you to defer your income. Some of these plans include 401(k) plans, 403(b) plans, 457 plans and Roth 401(k) plans. Without going into the rules of each of these plans, they are designed to encourage you to save for your retirement, when you are ready to hang up your "hustle-for-a-dollar" shoes. Because you are deferring your income in these plans and delaying the tax, if you decide to take the money out before you reach 59.5 years old, you will have to pay "Uncle Sam" and pay a penalty (this is the general rule). Never do this unless you are absolutely backed up against a wall! This is why we create other buckets of money so that you do not have to dip into this bucket until later in life.

Please, please, please find out if your employer makes any matching contributions to your plan. If they do make matching contributions, you need to make sure you meet their match. Making a matching contribution is more important than you buying a share of stock to place in your middle bucket. Why, you might ask? It's free money!

LONG-TERM BUCKET EXAMPLES

EMPLOYER SPONSORED
RETIREMENT PLANS

IRA

ROTH IRA

SEP IRA

REAL ESTATE

The Guarantee Bucket

In the field of finance, the word "guarantee" is a hush-hush word. Advisors and planners are afraid to use it, and they should be, quite frankly. If you are speaking to clients about investing, there aren't any guarantees. There are, however, areas in the field where you can say guarantee. The guarantee bucket represents those items in our financial house where we get and can create guaranteed income during our lifetime.

Let's start with the obvious: Social Security retirement income. To qualify for this guaranteed retirement check our government has promised to pay us, a worker must be fully insured. To become fully insured, you must have earned at least forty quarters of coverage. The quarter of coverage is an amount in wages subject to Social Security. The longer you wait to draw this check, the larger your check will be, and depending on the year of your birth, you could get additional increases in your monthly benefit up to the age of seventy. If you start taking Social Security early at the age of sixty-two, your benefits will be reduced.

While I label Social Security a guarantee, there are some caveats. Some of us will definitely receive Social Security benefits as a guaranteed payment backed by our government. The full retirement age for anyone born 1960 and later is sixty-seven years of age. I fall into this age range. This payment may be a guarantee for some of us, but not all of us may be lucky enough to receive the benefit. According to an editorial from *Investor's Business Daily*, "The latest Trustee Report released from the Social Security Administrations says that Social Security can meet its financial obligations for about 18 more years. After that, the trust fund will be exhausted, and payroll taxes won't cover nearly all the benefit costs."[14]

---

[14] "Social Security's Demise Is Much Closer Than You Think," Editorial, *Investor's Business Daily*, May 8, 2015, http://news.investors.com/ibd-editorials/050815-751813-study-finds-that-social-security-forecasts-too-optimistic.htm.

This news is bleak and should be a wakeup call for those who have relied solely on the hopes of Social Security to cover their retirement income. Ignorance is not bliss in the situation of Social Security because we have been forewarned for years about the strength of the fund. Prepare yourself now to fund your retirement cash flow on your own.

There have been suggested solutions to the declining Social Security system. One suggestion has been to raise the full retirement age. Another has been to reduce the amount of the benefit, which does not sit well with older voters. Whatever solution our government comes up with, we should not sit back and wait on a hope and a prayer that we will not be effected.

I encourage everyone to log on to the Social Security website and review your benefits statement. You can look at the history of how much you have paid into Social Security and see what your benefits would look like if you waited or started taking the money early. To save money, the administration stopped mailing out these documents some time ago, so you must go online to review.

What else can fall into the guarantee bucket? Pension income if you are still eligible. Many companies have steered clear of offering guaranteed pension plans to their employees and have opted for plans where employees contribute on their own and the funds aren't guaranteed by the employer such as a 401(k) plan or other defined contribution plans. But there are a few companies who still have them for their older, tenured employees. As a matter of fact, my former employer has recently sent out a mass mailing to all of their former employees offering a chance to take a lump sum amount or take the guaranteed pension payment once we reach a certain age. Now, I am not speaking for my former employer, but from a business standpoint, this opportunity can be a "win-win" for all involved, especially the company. Think about it. By offering lump sum payments, the company clears themselves from having to make guaranteed payouts to employees who may live pass the age of 100, which I certainly hope I do! This is clearly a win for any company who can convince their employees to take a lump sum of money. If you expect to live a long life, you may want to stick with the pension payment. There are many other considerations when making this decision that I will not get into.

The sad part about being offered a lump sum of money is some people will take the money, which was meant for retirement, and pay off bills or go out and buy themselves a shiny new car (I know a few people who bought themselves a new toy on wheels). Not only will they have to pay tax on the money, but they will also incur a penalty. A large sum of money in the hands of some people is a bad idea.

I am sure some of you are wondering if I made the decision to take the lump sum or guaranteed pension payment. I won't say. But I will say that your decision, if offered this choice, should depend on the amount offered and your personal circumstances. This is something you can talk about with your financial advisor.

Nonetheless, pension payments are guaranteed payments that help with cash flow during your retirement years. To an extent, we have little control over our pension payments and Social Security payments. These amounts are calculated based on our working years. They are fixed payments, and we cannot add to them or make them larger.

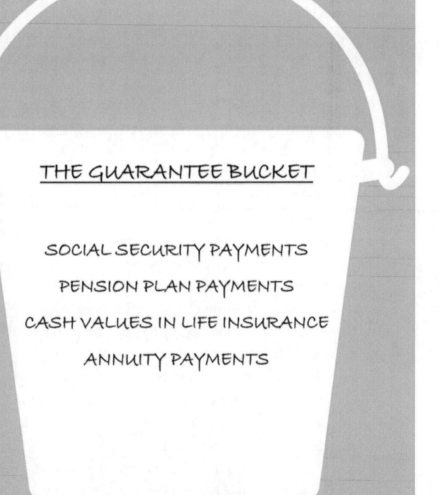

THE GUARANTEE BUCKET

SOCIAL SECURITY PAYMENTS

PENSION PLAN PAYMENTS

CASH VALUES IN LIFE INSURANCE

ANNUITY PAYMENTS

There are two other cash flow payments we can create to go in the guarantee bucket. These payments can come from the cash values in our life insurance policies and annuity payments from purchased annuities.[15]

The cash values in your whole life insurance policy can be a source of cash flow during your retirement years. In addition to the death benefit that is useful to your beneficiaries after you leave this earth, the money in these policies (if you have accumulated any) provides you with peace of mind as an additional source of funds if your other buckets are tied to the stock market in any way.

Let me paint a picture for you. What if you had created a strategy during retirement to make 4 percent distributions from your IRA tied into the market and the market dropped? This is a realistic scenario. Where do you go? Do you continue to withdraw from your account even when it is down? What if we have a repeat of the Great Recession? The cash value in your life insurance policy provides you with another cash flow source when we are experiencing a down market. No, you do not have to limit it to just that situation, but it can be a good one for the circumstances.

The cash value and death benefit mentally gives you permission to spend down your assets during your lifetime knowing that you have a death benefit that will provide a legacy for your loved ones once you have gone to glory. This is something that cannot be done with a term life insurance policy. Quite frankly, most people will outlive the term on their policy. I will stop here with this explanation and allow you to address the ends and outs of these policies with your personal advisor. They will help you determine what is best for your situation.

I know a woman who isn't currently living her life in her retirement years the way she imagined because she is trying to leave an inheritance to her children. Instead of using the money she accumulated in her

---

[15] Annuity contract guarantees are guaranteed solely by the strength and claims-paying ability of the issuer. Life insurance guarantees are based on the payment of required premiums and the claims paying ability of the issuer.

working years, she is saving it and trying to create three equal buckets of cash money for her children and a smaller bucket for her grandchildren. This woman has a very small life insurance policy and at her age, she is too old to purchase what she would like to leave behind for her children. Mentally, she does not have permission to spend down her assets. She shared with me that she wished she had purchased more life insurance when she was young. Now she cannot afford to purchase more because of her age and her fixed income.

Annuities are another source of guaranteed income. When you win the lottery and elect not to take the lump sum payout, the lottery system pays you an annuity payment for the rest of your life. You can create your own annuity and quite a few people do just that by rolling over their retirement funds into an annuity. An annuity can be a fixed or variable amount that is usually paid to an individual for the rest of her life. Annuities are usually backed by insurance companies.

Steady income gives many people peace of mind. You must weigh all of your options and look at your circumstances before you make this decision to place any of your retirement funds in an annuity. Too many media personalities have given annuities a bad name and painted a broad brush picture for all of society. Everything is relative, including the fees associated with annuities. As a disclaimer, I must explain that I own an annuity myself, which is an asset in my guarantee bucket.

Diversification is so important in wealth building. Having more than one option of cash flow is vitally important. We live in a volatile digital world, and our money is constantly moving at different rates. Accumulating a ton of cash is good but not the best way to build wealth. Cash loses purchasing power so we must fill multiple buckets to keep up with the rate of inflation.

I have found that my multiple bucket method works. I began using this method even when I didn't have a name for it when I started investing right out of college. Because of this method of wealth building, I have been able to withstand a layoff from work without skipping a beat in my household finances. My family and I managed to get through what I thought would be a financial crisis and a major change in lifestyle. But by the grace of God and my multiple money buckets, we weathered through our mini-storm.

My hope is that I reach young professional women and encourage them to adopt this method of investing. They have a chance to make it. They have such great opportunities to be wealth builders. All the cards are stacked in their favor. We must learn to maintain what we have and resist the temptation for immediate gratification with things that hold no value. I truly believe that when we are able to handle the small things in life, we are blessed with more things to handle. Learn to fill your buckets one at a time, taking baby steps. If you have the income, you have no excuse and the sky is the limit for you.

What's in your current buckets?

Short-term:

_____

_____

_____

_____

Midterm:

_____

_____

_____

_____

Long-term:

_____

_____

_____

_____

Guarantee:

_____

_____

_____

_____

NOTES

NOTES

Chapter 5
Protecting Your Buckets

I WOULD BE REMISS IF I DIDN'T DISCUSS THE IMPORTANCE OF PROTECTING your financial house. We need to make sure we do not have any leaks in our roof. In the event that something should happen to us, how will we preserve and keep our assets safely guarded? We protect them, of course, with insurance.

People who have accumulated wealth realize that stuff happens. This is why they don't personally finance themselves against risk, they use insurance. Most people would feel extremely uncomfortable driving a car without insurance for fear of getting in a car accident and being at fault (besides that it is illegal to drive without insurance). An accident could cost you dearly and wipe you out financially.

Remember that the potential for bankruptcy is always lurking around the corner and could be triggered from multiple sources. Unprotected at-fault car accidents, divorce, death of the household breadwinner, and disability can all unexpectedly strike. I like looking at insurance as a roof that covers our financial house. Our roof protects us from storms, just like insurance can protect us from the many storms we may weather throughout our lifetime. All days aren't sunny, and clouds will lurk.

I will look at a few areas under protection that I think are vitally important. Before I start, make sure you have the right team of people on hand to help you get your protection documents in place. Think about finding a good team that consists of an attorney, a CPA, and a financial advisor. They all work together and specialize in various areas that will surely help you with patching up any leaks you have in your roof, like having a will in place. There's a specialist for all income types. The internet is a great place to start, but the best place to start is through a friend. Referrals are great, and I am sure the specialist would appreciate the business.

Company Benefits

Many companies offer basic benefits to their employees, such as short-term disability and a basic fifty-thousand-dollar life insurance policy. Most benefits beyond this will have to come out of your pocket. You'll have to pay for the coverage. Take advantage of any free benefits your company offers that will not require an out-of-pocket expense. I will caution you that in most cases, if you leave your employer, your benefits are also left behind. This is a precautionary measure that everyone should be aware of. Unfortunately, in many cases, this is the only coverage some households have and I am here to tell you that it is not enough, especially if you can afford to get more outside of your employer.

I have heard horror stories of people working on their job for years and never purchasing any sort of insurance outside of their employer. When they finally left, voluntarily or by force, they could not qualify for any benefits. They waited until they were old or other morbidity issues kicked in and they simply could not afford any outside coverage. This is a sad situation to find yourself in so take measures to prevent it from occurring.

The best advice I can give you and anyone with questions about company benefits is that you should never rely solely on your employer for all of your benefits. We no longer live in an era where people remain on their jobs until they retire. Those days are over. According to data from the 2014 Bureau of Labor Statistics, the median number of years that wage and salary workers remain with their current employer is 4.6 years.[16]

---

[16] "Employee Tenure Summary," *Bureau of Labor Statistics*, Sept. 18, 2014, http://www.bls.gov/news.release/tenure.nr0.htm.

I have to share a story with you about this very topic. I had a couple come and see me to inquire about my services. We briefly discussed company benefits. I explained that if they never see me again, the one piece of advice I wanted them to take is not to rely on company benefits for all of their coverage. The wife was not very happy with my statement. Not only did she roll her eyes at me, but she proceeded with a long explanation that her employer had never gone through a layoff and that she was secure in her employment. Needless to say, she did not become a client, and she never came back to my office.

Fast forward six months later. I attended a baby shower and guess who I ran into. You guessed it, the young woman who rolled her eyes at my comments about company benefits. This conversation, however, was a lot smoother and pleasant compared to our first encounter. She shared with me that shortly after our meeting, she did not lose her job, but her husband did and her employer went through a restructuring process. During the restructuring process, she had to make tough decisions about her future with the company. She actually said, "You were right." But I did not say, "I told you so."

Disability Insurance

Everyone who relies on their paycheck to make a living needs disability insurance. As a matter of fact, if you are young and healthy, you are far more likely to need disability insurance than life insurance, especially if you have no dependents. Disability insurance is what I like to call paycheck protection because it protects your most important asset: your ability to make a living for yourself. Despite the importance of DI, most people aren't as familiar with its benefits compared to life insurance or they think they are invincible and nothing will ever happen to them, so they don't bother with purchasing the coverage.

Many healthy individuals will say, "I work out, and I am healthy. I don't want to waste my money on DI. I would rather buy a life insurance policy." Death is one of the guarantees in life, so I suppose they are betting on the guarantee. Unfortunately, risking the possibility of not being able to take care of regular expenses in the event of an untimely event such as a fall, hospitalization, or any accident that keeps you out of the work environment longer than ninety days could bankrupt you. Hospital expenses are one of the many reasons people file for bankruptcy in this country. They cannot cover medical bills along with other living expenses. This does happen, and no one is immune to it.

If you have no coverage at all on your job (short- or long-term disability) make sure you have ninety days of living expenses set aside. Long-term disability will kick in usually after ninety days. The longer you extend this period (referred to as your deductible period), the less your policy will cost. For example, a one-hundred-eighty-day elimination period will cost you less than a ninety-day elimination period (the time you must wait before the insurance kicks in).

Disability insurance will not cover 100 percent of your paycheck, but does cover up to 60 percent or more. If you never get better, you could possibly be paid 60 percent of your pay for the rest of your life. Covering only 60 percent of your pay is and should be an incentive for you to get back on your feet and back to work. If you have properly planned correctly, this policy could be a huge help in covering basic necessities during your disability.

There are many features and riders you can add to your policy that can be customized just for your needs, but those are beyond the scope of this text. Check around with companies and look at the features the policies have to offer. They are not all alike. The most important point is you need to make sure you are protecting your number one asset—you!

Life Insurance

I know insurance, especially life, is a touchy topic because people don't like to think about dying. Well, death is one guarantee that is surely going to happen whether you like it or not. Some people don't have a wakeup call until someone close to them dies without insurance in place or they have a near-death experience and realize that they need to get life insurance in a hurry.

Regardless of your income level or status, families face an uphill battle when they have to pay the bill to cover the funeral expenses of a family member who didn't care to make arrangements before their death. Heck, I've witnessed this in my own family. Even when you flip through the channels on television, you hear about the rich and famous who have estate issues that linger for years after their death because the deceased simply didn't plan properly.

I had one woman share with me that she received a phone call from a relative that she had not spoken to in years. The call was an invitation to attend a dinner. The woman was initially excited because she thought the family was trying to pull everyone together for old times' sake. She later found out in the conversation that a distant relative had died and the dinner was going to be used to pull family together to take up a collection to bury the cousin. Needless to say, this woman did not attend the dinner and was offended by the phone call. So much for family bonding!

When someone dies, families want to grieve. It's difficult to grieve when you are angry at the person who died. It saddens me when families have to go to the internet and ask strangers to donate to their GoFundMe account to cover funereal costs. Now, don't get me wrong. There are legitimate situations where people simply don't have the resources to cover the cost of life insurance because having food on the table and paying for living expenses are first priority. Those people get a pass. But I'm talking to those who place material lifestyle ahead of protection. These folks don't get a pass.

There are several types of life insurance policies that will fit many budgets. Your insurance professional can help you find one that is a perfect fit for your circumstances. If you feel you have no need for insurance because you are single and do not have dependents who will rely on your income after your death, make sure you have funds set aside to cover expenses in the—hopefully unlikely—event of your untimely demise.

Here's the bottom line regarding insurance. More women and children suffer and end up in poverty from the lack of life insurance in place. Women typically outlive their male spouses and if the male spouse is the sole breadwinner, how will the widow replace his income if he dies? Life insurance is one inexpensive way of making the family whole again after one spouse passes away. Make sure you purchase enough to provide for the surviving spouse during the grieving period and beyond.

Your company should not own all of your benefits!

Titling Your Assets

There will be people who will simply never create a will. Especially single people or those who feel they have no significant assets to leave behind. Everyone owns something, even if it's just the clothes on your back. They belong to you.

On a regular basis, I see new clients who have significant amounts of cash sitting in their bank accounts that have not been properly titled. When you ask if they have named a beneficiary on their checking or savings accounts, they look like they were just reminded to check something off of their to-do list. They give a deer-in-the-headlights stare.

If you own an individual bank account and have no desire to add a joint person to the account, make sure the account is set up as a POD

(Payable-On-Death) account. You usually see POD for bank accounts and TOD (Transfer-On-Death) for investment accounts. The beauty of POD/TOD accounts is they bypass probate and go directly to your named beneficiary by way of title. The titling on these accounts will also supersede what is written in a will.

Other accounts such as your 401(k) plans, life insurance, and your home can all pass to beneficiaries by way of title. Let me clarify by saying if you name a beneficiary on these accounts, they can bypass probate by way of title. In the case of your home, the title must be set as joint tenancy with rights of survivorship or tenancy by the entirety. Otherwise, it will have to be filed with the rest of your property in probate court. Make sure you review your beneficiaries annually when you review your documents.

With both POD and TOD accounts, you remain in control during your lifetime and can change the beneficiaries at any time. Wills can be contested and your intentions can be modified after death. With the titling of these accounts, there is no question or arguing about your wishes.

Don't forget to change the beneficiaries on all of your contracts (life insurance, annuities, banking, and investment accounts) if you go through a divorce. You often hear about ex-spouses arguing over assets after a death because the deceased spouse forgot to change the beneficiary on the accounts. The money or life insurance ends up being awarded to the ex-spouse because the titles were never changed on the account.

Wills and POA's

I will not go into the definition of a will because most people already know what it is. It isn't the definition of the will that is the problem; it is not having one that wreaks havoc on all of the assets you have accumulated during your lifetime. You build a solid financial house only to have it destroyed when you die. Take the time to get a will drawn up, especially if you have children. Decisions must be made about guardianship.

Determining who would be the caregiver of my children in the event of my untimely death was perhaps the strongest reason why my husband and I took so long to get our wills created. I hear this dilemma quite often when people give their excuse for not creating a will. Make your wishes known in writing because that is what you are doing when you create a will.

Additionally, a living will is not a will that goes into effect when you die, but a legal document summarizing your wishes regarding prolonging your life using medical treatment, such as a breathing machine. A living will is also referred to as an advance directive, healthcare directive, or a physician's directive. I personally would not want to live in a vegetative state and would not want my family spending thousands of dollars trying to keep me alive. Those are my wishes, and they have been documented in my living will. When medical wishes are not documented, family members are usually too emotional to make logical decisions about whether to pull the plug. Emotions can bankrupt a family!

For example, a case involving the daughter of a famous singer was played out in the Atlanta media. The young woman had been incapacitated for several months. The father and aunt of the child appeared to have a difference of opinion about her care. I often wondered if the child would have been pleased with the decisions her family made while she was too helpless to make them for herself.

A power of attorney (POA) is a written document authorizing someone else to represent or act on your behalf in private, business, or other legal matters. There are several types of powers you can grant the representative acting on your behalf which are beyond the scope of this book. These include durable, springing, and financial, just to name a few. If you suddenly become ill, leave the country, or simply need someone to step in on your behalf, it is a very good idea to put this in writing by granting powers. It's important that you set up the POA when you are of sound mind.

Many attorneys now include power of attorney and the drawing of a living will in packages they offer to clients. Just make sure you ask because there may be a different charge for this package versus only drawing up the basic will.

NOTES

NOTES

Chapter 6

If Money Wasn't an Object

THINK BACK TO WHEN YOU WERE IN KINDERGARTEN. YES, I KNOW YOU are probably thinking that kindergarten was a long time ago, and you probably feel like you cannot recall your kindergarten years. But give it a try. If that is too much of a stretch for you, try to think back as far as you can remember. What were you good at doing? I am sure a sibling or your parent could help you answer this question. Ask them what they thought you would do as an adult based on your skills as a young child.

What would you do for free if money wasn't an issue? This question has been posed by many writers who specialize in self-help books for people searching for a career or purpose. I can honestly say that in kindergarten I was good at counting, and I loved coordinating bright colors. My favorite pair of shoes was red patent leather Mary Janes. I wore them so much that I scuffed a hole in the toe of the shoes. Today, my home and wardrobe don't lack color, and I help people with their money for a living. I have provided both my decorating skills and my financial skills for free, and it never felt like work.

We are filled with a wealth of God-given talents that are bursting to come out. I love the quote, "The two most important days in your life are the day you are born and the day you find out why." Why have you been placed on this earth? You have a skill and talent that is uniquely yours.

I believe our greatest wealth potential is in our God-given talents. Wealth goes far beyond money. The wealth of knowledge and skills that reside within us will help us create all the money we need. It is left up to us to tap into ourselves and rebirth these skills we so uninhibitedly displayed in kindergarten!

Part of the entire process of building wealth and filling your buckets is learning who you are and where you want to be in the future. The desire of a future filled with peace and contentment should help us change our ways and habits.

Take some time out of your week, out of your day, and think about your inner "it," the one thing that you love doing, the one skill you are good at doing, that inner "it" that provides you a wealth of joy. Some of us have more than one thing that provides joy, but I do believe we are truly born with absolutely one single talent that we are good at like no other. It pulls at you like no other. You may hate to admit it, but it does. We all have a bucket of wealth and skills that we should be sharing with the world. Find it.

What are your talents?

_____

_____

_____

_____

_____

_____

_____

_____

_____

NOTES

HELPFUL TIPS

Chapter 7

Terrell's Personal Top Ten Wealth-Building Tips

I HAVE PROVIDED MY TOP TEN LIST IN MORE THAN A DOZEN PRESEN-tations, and the feedback has overwhelmingly been positive, so I've decided to include the list here for your benefit. Here's the list of ten things that I have personally incorporated in my life that have kept me out of financial trouble and helped me fill my money buckets. Some of the items on my list can be debated, but they have worked for me and now I am in a position to share what the outcome has been based on years of following these tips. These tips will be a great place to insert your bookmark or dog-ear the page. Most of these tips I touched on throughout the book.

1. *Create a Spending Plan/Budget*

   I work and review my personal budget every month when I sit down to pay my bills. Believe it or not, it needs a little tweaking every month because something different always seems to be on the horizon, or I free up money in one area which allows me to use it in other areas of my life (i.e., add more to my investment bucket). Take out your calendar and do a little forecasting. Think about what is on the horizon and pencil it in your budget. If you have a spreadsheet, add a note and highlight. Setting the budget in January and forgetting about it will not cut the mustard. You should review your budget regularly. You may not need to consult it monthly, but you definitely must refer to it on a regular basis.

2. *Eliminate Credit Card Debt*

    This goes without saying. Find a way to get rid of credit card debt. I personally don't sleep well at night knowing I owe money to a credit card company. To be honest, I simply hate paying interest charges. I feel like I am giving away my money for unnecessary reasons. Interest charges can add up if you are not careful! Who likes giving money away unless it is for charity? Carrying credit card debt means you are giving away money which can be used in other useful ways.

3. *Record Credit Card Transactions Just Like a Debit Transaction*

    I warned you these were my personal tips, so this step may not work for everyone. I like writing out my charges in an old check register. Yes, I do monitor my accounts electronically, but I still like writing out what I have charged because it resonates better in my brain. Mental notes are better written down! I do not have to wait to get my credit card bill to remember my charges, I just flip out my old check register.

4. *Create an Emergency Fund*

    Just as sure as you are living, you will have an emergency. Try to be prepared for them even if you cannot financially cover the entire emergency. Build a six to nine month emergency fund.

5. *Pay Yourself First and Make It Automatic*

    Most people save last, invest last, and build wealth last, after they have paid the bills and gone shopping. Change the order of your behavior if you are guilty of this habit. I have my savings on automatic contributions. If I have extra money after my automatic contributions, then I add extra, but the initial contribution will come out of my account as an automatic draft.

6. *Make Your Investment Contributions Automatic as Well*

    Remember, if times get tough and saving and investing becomes too much for your budget, you can always turn off your automatic contributions. If you get a raise, give your investment contributions a raise as well. Do this, of course, after you have built your emergency fund.

7. *Delay Gratification*

    I have become better at this as I have aged. Waiting takes practice and patience. I learned that I can wait, and if I wait, I may realize that I don't need whatever it is I thought I wanted. We live in a world where everything must happen now, now, now. We want immediate gratification. It's okay to wait. You become wiser and stronger when you pause, think, and wait. Take the old school route and save for an item. Waiting provides clearer and calmer thoughts to prevail, which allows you to make a more rational decision on anything!

8. *Save enough to Place a 20 Percent Down Payment on Your Home and Finance over Fifteen or Twenty Years*

    This statement causes debate among colleagues and in any discussion you have on wealth building: Should you pay off your mortgage early? If you do a web search on the subject matter, you will find arguments on either side about whether you should finance your mortgage over fifteen or thirty years. You even find arguments stating that you should place as little as possible on a down payment and use the difference for investing. To be honest, I personally have heard the notion of stretching out your mortgage for thirty years from those who have never paid off a mortgage. Have you ever heard anyone who has paid off their mortgage early complain or have regrets over this accomplishment? I haven't.

    My husband and I did place a 20 percent down payment on our home. We decided it would be our last move. We built the house we wanted and thought about what it would feel like living in our home when we were old. We decided to add our master bedroom on the main floor in the event we could not climb the stairs in our mature years. The thought of having a mortgage during retirement didn't make me feel well on the inside. I wanted my mortgage payment to be used for traveling during my retirement years. We started out with a thirty-year mortgage, then we went and re-financed later for fifteen years. Now that we are close to paying off the mortgage, one of our biggest regrets is not starting with the fifteen-year mortgage from the beginning of the financing process. We would be mortgage free by now. I am very excited about the thought of being mortgage free!

9. *Make Insurance Protection Your First Investment*

As a mother and wife, I sleep better at night knowing my family is protected if tragedy strikes. Sudden deaths, injuries, etc. can result in the collapse of your household. Protect your family; protect your loved ones. Having life insurance in place was a must when I became a mother. Talk about restless nights. In addition to life insurance, I purchased a customized disability policy in the event that I encountered a long-term disability. For single breadwinners, having disability on board is extremely important.

10. *Find Yourself a Good Advisor or Financial Mentor*

If I cannot find the answer to a question, I ask. Even the best of us don't hold the key to the magic box of knowledge. We should always be open to learning and listening to those who are experts in their field. Advisors can prevent you from financial failure. Take the time to ask questions. My financial mentors are just a phone call or text message away. I want to make sure I weigh my options before I act. Even advisors have advisors.

NOTES

EPILOGUE

Lessons for Generations

Things that have a common quality ever quickly seek their kind.
—*Marcus Aurelius*

YOU NEVER REALIZE THE IMPACT A PARENT HAS ON A CHILD UNTIL THEY become an adult. Growing up, I thought my mother was extremely tough on my siblings and me. She told us "no" more often than I care to remember, but I survived and perhaps became a better, stronger person because of my mother's no-nonsense guidance. I learned to live without all the unnecessary stuff. She shared with me that she felt she had to be tough because she was playing the double role of mother and father. Writing this book made me realize that so much of what I know about the discipline of saving money came from my mother.

Tough love was the only way my mother felt would keep us grounded. She said if you want something, make it happen on your own. And that's what I did and had to do. I didn't get a car until I purchased one on my own. She never cosigned anything for my sister or me. I used public transportation to go back and forth to work in high school and caught a ride with friends when I went off to college.

My mother believed in the importance of education, and she grew up thinking that if you had the chance to go to school and go to college, you would land a good job and your life would be quite fine. She often repeated the phrase, "Go to school, get a good education, and find yourself a good job." She believed this would solve all of the household financial problems in the world. At least it felt like it to me because she repeated the saying so often. Going to school and college was something she could not do growing up in a large family of ten children, because she had to help with the rearing of her younger brothers and sisters. I am a first generation college graduate on my mother's side of the family. I suppose her preaching worked.

My college years were not a cakewalk. My feet were my main mode of transportation. I walked to the nearby Piggly Wiggly just off the college campus to purchase my groceries. I remember just like it was yesterday, carrying my grocery bags up the hill back to my dorm room. I had no transportation and used the wheels God gave me. My mother said, "You will appreciate the car more if you get it on your own," which I eventually did, and she was absolutely correct in her assessment. I purchased a brand new Honda Accord when I graduated from college and landed my first job at the bank. The Honda Corporation did not require a co-signer at the time for recent college graduates who showed proof that they had a job. My offer for employment was all it took to get my car!

I am filled with emotions because I didn't realize her impact until I started writing. It doesn't take a PhD to educate a child. Loving them and wanting the best for them rubs off. Children watch their parents. We influence them and never know the impact we are having on them. Our spending habits rub off on them. If a child grows up watching their mother or father blow all of their money on what they feel are the finer things in life, don't be surprised if the child is the same way as an adult. Occasionally, you will have that one child who wants to be the opposite of his or her parents, but for the most part, the apple doesn't fall far from the tree, and the parents' habits become the habits of their offspring. Watch what you do around your children.

Monthly, as a child, I watched my mother sit at the coffee table, pull out her legal pad, and add up her bills (she still does this today). She never used a calculator, which would probably confuse her now if you showed her how to operate one. She always said to me, "Terrell, make sure you always put away something, even if it is only a dollar." I listened and took mental notes.

She taught me patience and the power of waiting. There is no immediate need for frivolous things. She gave me a wealth of knowledge that I can pass along to my children and others who care to listen.

She focused her thoughts and advice toward my sister and me. She felt like it would be a little harder for us to make it in this harsh world as women. That is what she saw growing up. Life was much harder for women than men. She watched her mother struggle, raising ten children without a consistent husband, so she told my sister and me to always keep a "little stash of cash to the side," just in case we were alone and didn't have support from our spouse. She didn't bash men because she felt very fortunate and blessed to marry her childhood sweetheart, my father. Her goal was to make sure her girls could survive, even if we never married.

I personally don't recommend hiding money from your spouse if you are married, but I do think women should be in control of their habits and behavior around money. My mother's spending habits and behavior with money rubbed off on me. Her apple stayed pretty close to the tree.

Thank you, Mama.

What lessons will you leave the next generation?

_____

_____

_____

_____

_____

_____

_____

_____

_____

_____

_____

_____

_____

_____

_____

_____

_____

_____

_____

_____

Appendix A

Common Monthly Expenditures & Outflows

Asset Building	Asset Building
Savings Investing Retirement Contribution	
Fixed Expenditures	**Fixed Expenditures**
Mortgage Auto Insurance Auto Payment Health Insurance Dental Insurance Life Insurance Disability Insurance Long Term Care Insurance Homeowners Insurance (Sometimes included in mortgage payment)	

Property Taxes (Sometimes included in mortgage payment) Student Loan Payment Credit Card Payments (Variable) Fixed Loan Payments	
Living Expenses (Discretionary and Non-discretionary) Association Dues Auto Fuel Auto Maintenance Cable/Internet Charity/Tithing Child Care Child Support Clothing Purchase Dry Cleaning Clubs/Organizational Memberships Entertainment (Movie Rental, Concerts, Plays…etc.) Food/Dining Out Food/Groceries Gifts (Birthdays, Weddings, Holiday) Hobbies Home Improvement/Home Maintenance	**Living Expenses (Discretionary and Non-discretionary)**

Living Expenses (Discretionary and Non-discretionary) cont.	Living Expenses (Discretionary and Non-discretionary) cont.
Home Lawn Care Home Security Homeowners Association Dues Maid/Cleaning Service Medical/Dental Co-Pays Medical Prescriptions Nanny Personal Grooming (Hair Nails) Pet Care Professional Fees/License Subscriptions Telephone/Mobile Travel Utilities (Electric) Utilities (Gas) Utilities (Water) Utilities (Sanitation) Travel (Work) Vacation Miscellaneous/Other Expenses	

NOTES

Appendix B

Personal Balance Sheet

Personal Balance Sheet

Assets

Cash & Cash Equivalent
Savings Bank Accounts
Money Market Accounts
CD</= 12 Months

Investment Assets

IRA
Brokerage Account
Retirement
Mutual Funds
CD>/= 12 Months

Personal Use Assets

Car
House
Jewelry
Furniture

Total Assets

Liabilities

Secured Loans
Home Loan
Car Loan

Unsecured Loans

Education Loan
Personal Loan
Credit Card Debt

Other Payables

Loan from family/friends
Other Dues

Total Liabilities

Assets - Liabilities = Net Worth

NOTES

Appendix C
Debt Ratios

Consumer debt payments should not exceed 20% of NET income

- **Housing debt** should be less than or equal to **28% of Gross income**
- Housing plus all other recurring debt should be less than or equal to **36% of Gross income**

Housing -28% Ratio

- $\underline{\text{Monthly Housing Cost (P+I+T+I)}}$ **
  Monthly Gross Income

Housing and All Other Debt Ratio -36% Ratio

- $\underline{\text{Monthly Housing Costs (P+I+T+I) + All Other Recurring Debt Payments}}$
  Monthly Gross Income

Emergency Fund

- **3-6 (6-9) months in nondiscretionary expenses in an emergency fund**
- **Nondiscretionary expenses include only those expenses that do not go away if you lose your job, such as mortgage, utilities, food, car loan, property taxes and insurance premiums**
- **Nondiscretionary expenses do not include income taxes, payroll taxes and contributions to a retirement savings account.**

** P+I+T+I (Principle+ Interest + Taxes +Insurance)

NOTES

Bibliography

Copeland, Larry. "Life Expectancy in the USA Hits a Record High." *USA Today*, Mar. 1, 2015. http://www.usatoday.com/story/new/nation/2014/10/08/us-life expectancy-hits-recor-high/16874039.

Elliott, Diana B. and Tavia Simmons. "Marital Events of Americans: 2009." *United States Census Bureau*, Aug. 2011. https://www.census.gov/prod/2011pubs/acs-13.pdf.

"Employee Tenure Summary." *Bureau of Labor Statistics*. Sept. 18, 2014. http://www.bls.gov/news.release/tenure.nr0.htm.

Hicken, Melanie. "Why Many Retired Women Live in Poverty." *CNN Money*, May 13, 2014, http://money.cnn.com/2014/05/13/retirement/retirement-women/.

Kimbro, Dennis P. *The Wealth Choice: Success Secrets of Black Millionaires*. New York, NY: Palgrave Macmillan, 2013.

Parker, Kim and Eileen Patten. "The Sandwich Generation: Rising Financial Burdens for Middle-Aged Americans." *Pew Research Center*, Jan. 30, 2013. http://www.pewsocialtrends.org/2013/01/30/thesandwichgeneration/.

Phelan, Donna M. "Women's New Retirement Conversation." *Retirement and Good Living*, Feb. 17, 2015. http://retirementandgoodliving.com/womens-news-retirement-conversation/.

Raghavan, Divya. "How The Gender Pay Gap Harms Women's Retirement." *Forbes*, Nov. 12, 2014. http://www.forbes.com/sites/nextavenue/2014/11/12/how-the-gender-pay-gap-harms-women.

Scott, Cindy. "Meeting the Financial Planning Needs of Women Clients." WealthManagement.com, Jan. 23, 2014. http://wealthmanagement.com/viewpoints/meeting-financial-planning-needs-women-clients.

"Social Security's Demise Is Much Closer Than You Think." Editorial. *Investor's Business Daily*, May 8, 2015. http://news.investors.com/ibd-editorials/050815-751813-study-finds-that-social-security-forecasts-too-optimistic.htm.

Stanley, Thomas J. *The Millionaire Next Door*. Lanham, MD: Taylor Trade Publishing, 2010.

Tarantine, Ruth A. *Against All Odds: How to Move from Provider-Centered Care to Patient-Centered Care*. Pittsburgh, PA: inCredible Messages Press, 2014.

Tarantine, Ruth. "The Sandwich Generation: Who Is Caring for You?" *The Huffington Post*, Sept. 7, 2014. http://www.huffingtonpost.com/ruth-tarantine-dnp-rn/baby-boomers-caregivers_b_5733782.html.

About the Author

TERRELL DINKINS IS A FINANCIAL ADVISOR,
wealth empowerment speaker, and author.
As an advisor, she has a tremendous passion
for creating intelligent financial strategies that
help individuals, families, and small business
owners reach their personal financial goals.
Maximizing wealth potential and minimizing
costs and inefficiencies are key goals Terrell
aims for with all of her clients.

She has been featured in numerous magazines, sat on panels, and
spoken to numerous groups, providing her expert opinion on personal
finance and sharing her knowledge on getting your financial house
in order. She has traveled international waters, speaking to audiences
on wealth building.

Terrell is a true "Georgia Peach" through and through. She is a native
Atlantan and received her BBA from Georgia Southern University,
her MBA from Mercer University's Stetson School of Business and
Economics in Atlanta, and completed the executive program for Financial Planning from the University of Georgia's Terry College of
Business. She is a wife and mother of two children and a proud member
of Alpha Kappa Alpha Sorority, Incorporated.

Follow One Bucket Nation on:

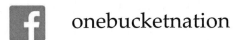 onebucketnation

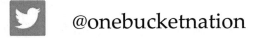 @onebucketnation

 #onebucketnation

Available on:

Amazon.com

Shop.BookLogix.com

OneBucketNation.com